FINISHING WOOD

EDITORS OF **FINE WOODWORKING**

The Taunton Press

THE TAUNTON PRESS, INC.
63 South Main Street, PO Box 5506
Newtown, CT 06470-5506
E-mail: tp@taunton.com

EDITORS: Peter Chapman, Christina Glennon
COPY EDITOR: Diane Sinitsky
INDEXER: Jim Curtis
JACKET/COVER DESIGN: Guido Caroti
INTERIOR DESIGN: Carol Singer
LAYOUT: Susan Lampe-Wilson
COVER PHOTOGRAPHERS: Front cover: Mark Schofield, except top center Michael Pekovich
Back cover: Mark Schofield left and right, Jonathan Binzen center

Fine Woodworking® is a trademark of The Taunton Press, Inc., registered in the U.S. Patent and Trademark Office.

The following names/manufacturers appearing in *Finishing Wood* are trademarks: 3M™; Abralon®; Accuspray™; Aqua Coat®; Bear-tex®; Blendal®; Bloxygen®; Briwax®; Butcher's®; Cabot®; Crown®; Crystalac®; Dawn®; Deft®; Earlex®; Formby's®; Fre-Cut™; Gator®; General Finishes®; Goddard's®; Graco®; Hope's®; Klean-Strip®; LakeOne™; M.L. Campbell®; Master's Blend™; Milwaukee®; Mini-Mite 3™; Minwax®; Mirka®; Mirlon Total®; Mixol®; Murdoch's Hard Sealer™; Old Masters®; Phoenix Finish-All™; Plastic Wood®; Pore-O-Pac™; Pratt & Lambert® 38®; Preval®; Rockhard™ Table Top Varnish; Rockler®; Rubio® Monocoat; SandBlaster™; SealCoat™; Sherwin-Williams®; Shopsmith®; Solar-Lux™; Sutherland Welles®; Teflon®; Titan® Capspray™; Titebond®; TransTint®; Varathane®; Vaseline®; Velcro®; Wagner Flexio®; Watco®; Waterlox®; Woodcraft®; Zar®; Zinsser® Bulls Eye®

Library of Congress Cataloging-in-Publication Data

Title: Finishing wood / editors of Fine woodworking.
Other titles: Fine woodworking.
Description: Newtown, CT : Taunton Press, Inc., [2017] | Includes index.
Identifiers: LCCN 2017025331 | ISBN 9781631868931
Subjects: LCSH: Wood finishing.
Classification: LCC TT325 .F5296 2017 | DDC 684/.084--dc23
LC record available at https://lccn.loc.gov/2017025331

Printed in the United States of America
10 9 8 7 6 5 4 3 2 1

ABOUT YOUR SAFETY: Working wood is inherently dangerous. Using hand or power tools improperly or ignoring safety practices can lead to permanent injury or even death. Don't try to perform operations you learn about here (or elsewhere) unless you're certain they are safe for you. If something about an operation doesn't feel right, don't do it. Look for another way. We want you to enjoy the craft, so please keep safety foremost in your mind whenever you're in the shop.

ACKNOWLEDGMENTS

Special thanks to the authors, editors, art directors, copy editors, and other staff members of *Fine Woodworking* who contributed to the development of the chapters in this book.

Contents

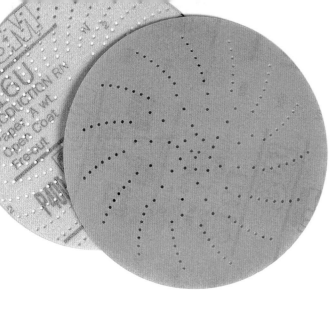

Introduction

For many woodworkers, finishing a project is like a journey to a mysterious land, one that's chock full of pitfalls, magic potions, and looming treachery. But after you've spent hours and hours of hard work on your project, the last thing you want to do is fly blind. You need a good map.

Well here it is. *Finishing Wood* is a collection of the best articles on finishing, taken from the pages of *Fine Woodworking* magazine. Here you'll get all the information you need to pick and apply the perfect finish for your project.

Finishing Wood covers all the bases, from the basics and beyond. Start by understanding the common terms and why wood needs a finish, and learn about all the finishes available—including when they go bad. You'll also learn why surface prep is the most important part of the job. After all, a finish is meant to enhance the wood, and it will do the same for any defects left behind.

You'll get tips and techniques for applying the most common finishes, including shellac, polyurethane, oil, wax—even soap! Plus you'll get professional advice on the best ways to color wood. And if you're looking for ways to finish fast, you'll find it all in the spraying section of the book, which includes expert buying advice and techniques that will guarantee success.

So don't fly blindly into your finishing steps. Get all the finishing info you need right here, and complete your masterpiece with the perfect one.

Have fun in the shop!

Tom McKenna
Editorial Director, *Fine Woodworking*

Why Finish Wood?

MARK SCHOFIELD

Finishing experts tell you how to apply a finish, but they never explain *why* you should finish wood. Why not leave a piece in its just-planed state showing the wood's natural beauty? Is it really necessary to go to all that trouble coating your piece with some combination of oil, resin, or plastic?

In fact, there are many important reasons for applying a finish—some aesthetic and some practical. A finish can reduce seasonal movement and the resulting stresses on joinery. It also makes a surface more impact-resistant and protects wood from everyday use, whether the piece is a rarely handled picture frame, a kitchen table, or an outside chair. Also, the right combination of dyes, stains, and clear finishes can turn humdrum wood into an eye-catching piece.

And finally, there *are* some occasions when no finish really is a valid option.

Some finishes slow wood movement

When it comes to protecting a piece of furniture from the damage that can be caused by wood movement, applying a finish is no substitute for careful construction.

Still, certain finishes will reduce wood's tendency to absorb and release moisture. This in turn will slow seasonal expansion and contraction, reducing stresses that can eventually damage joinery, helping to minimize

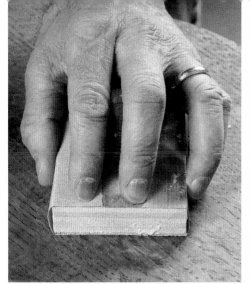
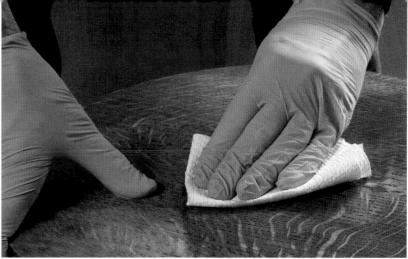

An oil finish is easily renewed. Penetrating finishes like linseed oil or tung oil don't protect as well as film finishes, but they can be sanded away to repair damage and then renewed.

problems like door panels that rattle in winter or drawers that stick in summer.

Some finishes are better at this than others (see the chart at right). No clear finish can match paint at controlling moisture, even over a couple of weeks. Pure oil finishes in particular are ineffective. Spar varnish gives some protection, but the standouts among clear finishes are shellac and polyurethane.

If you do apply an effective moisture-excluding finish, be sure to treat all surfaces equally. Otherwise, each side of the surface will absorb and release moisture at a different rate, causing the boards to cup.

Finished wood stays cleaner

No piece stays looking like the day it was made. The surface gets a slightly rough feeling, sunlight oxidizes the surface cells, and hands leave oil and dirt. A clear finish can give wood varying degrees of protection against environmental damage as well as everyday wear and tear.

The need for protection varies by the intended location and use of the piece. If you want the look of natural wood, a rarely handled piece such as a picture frame or an ornamental turning probably only needs a single coat of finish followed by a coat of wax. That's enough to allow dust to be wiped off and not into the grain.

No Finish Is Waterproof

If you live where there are wide humidity swings between winter and summer, you should weigh moisture control more heavily in choosing a finish. Use this chart to compare the moisture-repelling properties of common finishes. Each finish was applied in three coats on samples of clear Ponderosa pine. The test pieces—along with unfinished control samples—were then kept in a controlled environment of 80°F and 90% humidity to simulate real-world humidity changes. Afterward, each was weighed and compared against its unfinished control piece to gauge relative water gain.

PERCENTAGE OF MOISTURE REPELLED			
Finish	1 day	7 days	14 days
Paste wax	17	0	0
Linseed oil	18	2	0
Tung oil	52	6	2
Nitrocellulose lacquer	79	37	19
Spar varnish	87	53	30
Shellac	91	64	42
Oil-based polyurethane	90	64	44
Oil-based paint	97	86	80

Source: Forest Products Laboratory, U.S. Forest Service
Excerpted from *Understanding Wood* by R. Bruce Hoadley (The Taunton Press, 2000)

Reveal depth and beauty. A clear finish transforms the wood by enhancing contrast in the figure and emphasizing the surface luster.

Tiger maple, in living color. Dyes can give your work a full color palette while also enhancing figure.

Tabletops likely to come into contact with food and drink need a finish that can protect the wood. Unfinished, scrubbed-pine tables were fine for the nobles who employed scullery maids, but if you're cleaning up after yourself, you'll find that traces of red wine and ketchup are removed far more easily from a durable film finish such as varnish or polyurethane.

Penetrating finishes offer less protection, but minor damage can be repaired more easily by sanding and then wiping on another coat of finish. This easily repairable finish is suitable for surfaces that won't be subject to frequent damage by liquids. The "easily" is relative when compared to repairing a film finish: It is still quite a lot of work to sand out the damage and apply new finish to the damaged area and possibly the whole immediate surface, so you don't want to do this once a month to a kitchen table. Almost any other piece, including the tops of occasional tables (especially in an adults-only house), will be fine with a penetrating finish.

Enhance wood's beauty

Yes, beauty is in the eye of the beholder, but even those who hate finishing must have had that moment of pleasure when the first coat of finish lights up the wood. The impact is greatest with highly figured wood—burls, crotches, blister, and ribbon stripe. Finish increases the light/dark contrast and exaggerates the shimmer, or chatoyance.

Applying a finish also increases the contrast between light and dark woods, whether it is walnut drawer pulls, wenge trim, or the mahogany background to holly stringing.

Don't confine yourself to clear coats: Dyes can really put the tiger in tiger maple, while bright dyes help blister and quilt-figured maple to jump out.

Two ways to survive the great outdoors. To finish his outdoor furniture, Sean Clarke applies multiple layers of epoxy sealer and marine varnish (top). Or you could take Hank Gilpin's approach and apply no finish at all (above).

can wipe it with a cloth or a towel and you have a surface ready for those white trousers or dresses. An unfinished piece will stay damp for hours or even days after a good soaking and will grow lichen, moss, etc.

Outdoor finishes not only need to withstand the elements but also must allow for far more wood movement than interior finishes. The answer is to use a durable yet flexible finish. Apply many layers of a marine varnish, particularly on end grain. Immediately repair any damage before water can get under the finish, and when the surface loses its shine, apply another coat. If you wait until the finish has begun to crack and peel, the only solution is to go back to bare wood and begin again.

Easy option for tropical woods. Dense, oily woods like cocobolo absorb less moisture and can be sanded and buffed to a high polish.

Finishing outdoor furniture

Whether to finish an outside piece is rather like deciding whether to dye your hair. You can either accept going gray, or you can apply dye/finish on a regular basis. In both cases, make the choice and then stick with it; neither gray roots nor an outdoor piece with peeling finish are attractive.

A finished outdoor piece is much easier to keep clean and dry. After a day of rain, you

For those determined not to apply a finish, a durable outdoor wood such as teak, white oak, or cedar will give you years of good service before weathering starts to weaken it. You can also avoid finishing some dense, oily tropical hardwoods such as cocobolo or rosewood. Sand them to a high grit and then buff them (on a buffing wheel for small objects) and they'll retain a medium luster.

The Language of Finishing

MARK SCHOFIELD

One reason many woodworkers find finishing difficult may be because the language is so confusing. If your finish is bleeding, does it need time to cure? If it is blushing, should you be distressed (or perhaps you should be fuming)? Do you call the mob if you need a finish rubbed out?

Surface prep: the foundation of finishing

Surface preparation is the process of using handplanes, scrapers, and sandpaper (powered by machine or hand) to remove surface blemishes left by machines. A handplane and card scraper is the fastest method; sandpaper is typically the last step.

Almost all sandpaper now uses the European **FEPA scale** (a metric system for measuring the coarseness of the abrasive granules), denoted by a P before the number. The older **CAMI scale** is now mostly confined to grits higher than 600 in wet-or-dry paper used for sanding finishes.

Most random-orbit sanding disks (and some rolls of abrasive) come with a **hook-and-loop** backing (aka Velcro®) that can be pricey but lets you remove and reuse the disks. **Sanding swirls** and **pigtails** are visible scratches caused by pressing down too hard on a random-orbit sander. The sander's weight alone is enough to let the disk do its job and yet spin randomly, leaving an evenly distributed scratch pattern.

For a penetrating oil finish (see p. 10), you should sand up to P220-grit on most hardwoods, but on cherry or other woods that tend to absorb oil unevenly, I would go to P320- or even P400-grit to burnish the surface. For a thicker film finish, you can stop at P180-grit, but make sure the surface is flat and smooth. Check your progress with a spotlight or desk light just above the surface of the wood, shining across it. This is known as a **raking light**.

Finish sanding using a **sanding block**. This can be either solid cork, or wood faced with ⅛-in.-thick cork or rubber sheet (a cork floor tile works well). If you are applying a water-based dye or a waterborne clear finish to the bare wood, wet the wood with a damp cloth to **raise the grain**, causing the surface fibers to swell. Let the surface dry, and then hand-sand. This prevents the dye or clear finish from raising the grain and leaving a rough surface.

While you are hand-sanding, you'll want to **break the edge**s of the piece. This involves very slightly rounding or chamfering the sharp corners. This makes

Hook-and-loop

Pigtail

Surface preparation

Raking light

Breaking edges

Tack cloth

the edge feel better to the touch, helps resist dents, and is more forgiving under a film finish. Breaking the edge lets the finish flow around the corner, giving the whole surface an even coat.

When you've finished sanding, remove the dust with a vacuum cleaner, blow out any remaining dust in the wood's pores with compressed air, and then wipe the surface with a cloth dampened with denatured alcohol or with a **tack cloth**. This is a cheesecloth impregnated with a kind of sticky varnish to pick up any fine dust remaining on the surface. Unfold the cloth, then lightly bundle it and wipe the surface, applying minimal pressure. Pressing down hard can leave sticky residue on the surface that may interfere with waterborne finishes.

Oil-based finishes

Oil and oil-based clear finishes are the finishes that most *Fine Woodworking* readers use, but their complexity and range of variations also make them the most complicated to understand.

The simplest are **pure oil finishes**, which contain no resins or solvents. These are applied thinly and rubbed into the wood, eventually revealing any luster or **chatoyance** deep in the wood. Over time, pure oil finishes start to look dull but are easily cleaned and renewed.

The most common pure oil finish is **boiled linseed oil**, which is derived from the seeds of the flax plant. It is not actually boiled but has chemicals known as **metallic driers** added to speed up the absorption of oxygen, which is how an oil finish cures. **Raw linseed oil** contains no driers, will take far longer to dry, and will not cure as hard as boiled linseed oil.

Like boiled linseed oil, **pure tung oil** is another **drying oil**, meaning that it will dry to a hard finish and will not remain greasy or sticky.

Pure oil finish

Gel finish

Chatoyance

Wiping varnish

The range of **oil-based finishes** is immense, but they all share three components. The first is a **binder**, also known as a resin, which when dry forms a film attached to the wood's surface. Binders in oil-based finishes include **acrylic**, **phenolic**, **alkyd**, and **urethane**. The second component is a **carrier** to help the binder flow out. The most common are linseed, tung, and soybean oils. Finally, you need a **thinner** (a solvent) to achieve a workable viscosity. Commercial finishes use mostly **mineral spirits**, but shopmade oil-based finishes can be made with some **naphtha** for faster drying or **turpentine** for slower drying (and a nicer smell).

Varying the ratio of these three components creates different finishes. You'll sometimes hear a finish described as **short oil** or **long oil** as if it were a commodities trader. A short-oil finish will have a higher percentage of binder and will form highly protective indoor finishes such as varnish or polyurethane. Thinned with solvent, it becomes a **wiping varnish**, meaning it can be applied with a clean cotton cloth. A long-oil varnish, also known as **spar varnish**, has more oil to give it a more elastic consistency that can cope with the increased wood movement outdoors. A higher-quality spar varnish is a **marine-grade varnish**, which should contain **ultraviolet absorbers** or **inhibitors** to slow damage to the finish from sunlight. A diluted long-oil finish is known as **Danish oil**. It is poured on the surface and allowed to penetrate the wood, and then the surplus is wiped off.

Gel varnish, **gel polyurethane**, or simply **gel finish** are all oil-based finishes with a thickening agent. This makes them much less messy to wipe on and off.

The many types of shellac

Derived from the protective casing of a type of insect larvae in southern Asia, this ancient finish has been refined into various grades and sold in flake or granule form. Among

the least refined is **seedlac**, a reddish-orange granule mostly used in matching antique finishes.

Buttonlac comes in small coin-sized disks. Like seedlac, it contains about 5% wax, giving it a cloudy appearance. This makes it good for an antique look but less durable than grades of shellac that have been dewaxed. **Dewaxed** grades of shellac come in flakes and are described by their color, from a dark **garnet** through **ruby**, **orange**, and **lemon** to a very pale **blond**.

Shellac is an evaporative finish, where one coat melts into the prior one. Its viscosity is measured by its cut. When you dissolve 3 lb. of dry shellac in 1 gal. of **denatured alcohol** (ethanol with some methanol added to make it non-drinkable), you get a 3-lb. cut. To thin this to a more easily brushed 2-lb. cut, add one part alcohol to two parts liquid shellac by volume.

Shellac

Buttonlac

Blond

Orange

Garnet

Lacquer

Solvent-based lacquer

Lacquer is another evaporative finish. **Lacquer thinner** is made from several solvents blended in different combinations. Faster-evaporating thinner is used when spraying lacquer, but slower blends allow you to brush this finish.

The most commonly sprayed lacquer outside commercial operations is **nitrocellulose lacquer**, made from cotton cellulose, nitric acid, and other acids. It dries fast and offers great clarity and depth, but its high solvent content is highly air polluting. It

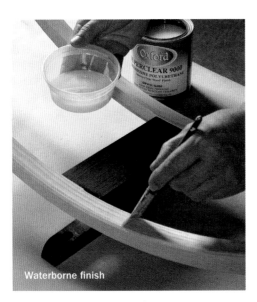

Waterborne finish

also has a strong yellow color, which increases as the finish ages. For a non-yellowing lacquer, go with **CAB-acrylic lacquer**, which is made with clear acrylic resin.

Waterborne finishes

Often incorrectly called water-based finishes (a true water-based finish would dissolve in water), **waterborne finishes** consist of acrylic and polyurethane resins mixed with glycol ether solvent and water. As the water evaporates, the solvent makes the resins sticky so that they come together in a continuous film, the definition of a **coalescing finish**.

Waterborne finishes have names like lacquer, polyurethane, and varnish, but are nothing like their solvent-based namesakes. Instead, they all have a white, milky appearance in the can, they dry almost colorless, and they clean up with water.

The right rag for a wipe-on finish

Wiping on a finish is a relatively simple process, but it's not without pitfalls. I wish I had a dollar for every finishing article I've read that suggests using a lint-free cotton cloth. Many cotton items from socks to underwear contain **lint**—residual flecks of fiber that gradually come loose and disappear after multiple washings. That's why an old, much-washed T-shirt makes a great application tool.

To check a cloth for lint, use it to dry a wine glass or clean a mirror with glass cleaner. Any lint will show up on the glass and will mar your project if you use a linty cloth to apply a finish.

Aside from lint marring a wiped-on finish, you may also encounter a problem known as **bleeding**. This occurs with oil finishes on open-pored woods such as oak when excess oil oozes from the pores long after you've

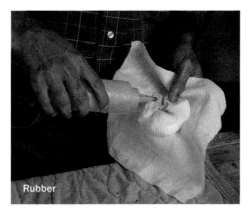
Rubber

French polish

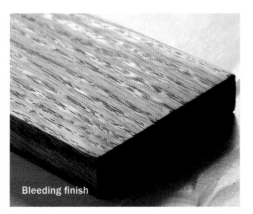
Bleeding finish

wiped the surface dry. If you don't repeatedly wipe the surface, these droplets will dry into small, shiny dots that you'll have to sand off.

One important wipe-on finishing technique is known as **French polishing**, in which a **rubber** (a pad made from several layers of cotton cloth) is used to apply the multiple thin layers of shellac that make up this classic finish.

Brush up your language skills

All brushes have **filaments**—the individual strands, natural or synthetic, that make up the body of the brush. Only a few, though, have **bristles**, a type of natural filament made from animal fiber. These are typically made from hog bristle, also known as China bristle because that is where the material comes from. Other fibers used in **natural-filament** brushes include ox hair and badger hair. All work well for oil-based finishes, shellac, or lacquer. The natural resilience of the fibers allows them to hold a lot of finish and distribute it evenly. Avoid using natural-filament brushes for waterborne finishes, however, because the filaments will absorb water and lose their resilience.

Synthetic filaments

Natural bristles

Flagging

Chisel end

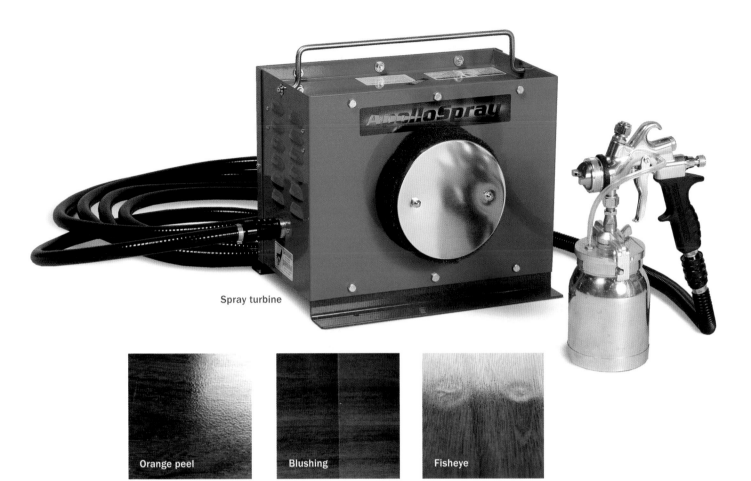

Spray turbine

Orange peel

Blushing

Fisheye

To apply waterborne finishes, use a brush with man-made filaments or **synthetic bristles**. These are mostly made from nylon or polyester. A particularly fine-strand filament is called **Taklon**; these types of brushes are great for applying a thin top-coat that leaves almost no brush marks. Synthetic-bristle brushes can also be used for other finishes, and many consider them almost as good as top-of-the-line natural-filament brushes.

Natural or synthetic, look for filaments that are split and frayed at the ends. A brush with this characteristic, known as **flagging**, leaves fewer brush marks. For the same reason, look for a **chisel-end** brush, where the filaments form a V at the end rather than being flat.

The metal that encloses the base of the filaments is known as the **ferrule**. On any brush you intend to keep, the ferrule should be made of brass or stainless steel to avoid rust that eventually can contaminate the finish.

Learn what to say before you spray

Spraying may leave a great finish, but learning all the terms makes it hard to get started. There are three areas you need to know about. The first is the source of compressed air for the spray gun, either a **turbine** (a self-contained unit with a built-in blower) or an air compressor. Both systems are defined as **HVLP** (high volume, low pressure). They use low air pressure to **atomize** the finish (turn it into tiny particles), so more of the finish stays

High gloss

Wet-sanding

Low luster

on the workpiece instead of bouncing off and ending up as **overspray**.

The last group of spraying terms has to do with the quality of the finish. Spraying is meant to speed up the finishing process, so you are aiming for an **off-the-gun** finish, one that needs no further work. Before you reach that nirvana, you will probably experience some problems. One of the most common is known as **orange peel** (see the photo on p. 15), a bumpy surface caused by too heavy a film or poor atomization of the finish. To fix it, you can cut back the supply of fluid and either increase the air pressure to the spray gun or reduce the viscosity of the finish.

Another problem when spraying fast-drying finishes such as lacquer or shellac on very humid days is **blushing**. This happens when water vapor gets trapped in the film of finish and creates a whitish haze. The solution is to add a blend of solvents known as a retarder to the finish to lengthen the drying time. A less-common problem is **fisheye**, small craters often caused by silicone contamination from old furniture polish or shop lubricants on the wood's surface.

Finishing the finish

Unless you are an expert sprayer, with any kind of built-up film finish you will probably need to work on the last coat after it has fully cured. There may well be small bits of dust known as **nibs** stuck in the finish; the surface may be marred by brush marks or perhaps small sags and runs on vertical surfaces. Or, you may not want a glossy appearance. The solution to all these problems is to rub out the finish using a variety of methods and fine abrasives.

Scuff-sanding

Steel wool

Auto polish

The shine on the surface is referred to as **sheen**, and is a measure of the amount of light it reflects. A **high-gloss** sheen, sometimes called a **piano finish**, requires careful leveling and polishing of the topcoat. A less formal **low-luster** finish is easier to achieve.

Any high-gloss finish must be perfectly flat, so the first step is to level it by **wet-sanding** with wet-or-dry sandpaper lubricated with water and a tiny amount of dish soap. With some finishes, you'll want to lightly **scuff sand** between coats to level the surface. If you sand through the topcoat of a finish like varnish where each coat doesn't melt into the previous one, you will create a **witness line**. The only way to cover up this ragged edge of finish is to apply another coat or two and start leveling again.

Final polishing of a high-gloss finish used to be done with **pumice**, a finely ground lava, lubricated with mineral oil, followed by **rottenstone**, a kind of limestone. These days, it is much easier to use polishing compounds and liquids formulated for polishing car bodies.

For a lower-sheen satin finish, rub the surface with 0000 (pronounced "4 ought") **steel wool** or a 4,000-grit **Abralon®** pad. This foam-backed abrasive disk works well on flat and curved surfaces. After that you can apply some furniture polish or paste wax and rub or buff it out with a lint-free cloth.

A Pro's Secret to a Perfect Finish

PETER GEDRYS

You may have admired the mirror finish on a piano or wondered how expert finishers get that dead-smooth clear coat on fine furniture. The secret isn't just in sanding or spraying but also in an intermediate step called grain, or pore, filling. Unfortunately, this step often gets eliminated because it can be messy, a bit time-consuming, and at times troublesome. But this single process can help transform a finish from mundane to spectacular.

I'll show you when to use a grain filler, why it shouldn't be used only on tabletops, and how to get the best results with the least mess. I'll also describe the pros and cons of five commercial brands of filler.

Oil-based vs. water-based fillers

Grain fillers come in oil-based and water-based varieties. Water-based fillers don't smell as strong as oil types, tool cleanup is easier, and they dry faster. This last feature, though, can be a double-edged sword. I like the fact that oil-based fillers take a little longer to dry because I can work on a larger area at a time. For example, when filling a mahogany desktop, I may be able to do it in

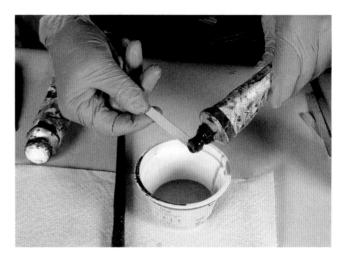

Mix the right color. Most of the fillers have to be colored to either match the wood or be slightly darker. For an oil-based filler, dilute some filler with mineral spirits, then add artist's oils until you reach the desired color. For mahogany, burnt umber is a good base color tweaked by adding black or red.

Add the color to the filler. Stir the colored concentrate into a slightly larger quantity of filler than you think you'll need. With oil-based fillers, the color concentrate adds 10% to 15% by volume; with water-based, 5% to 10%.

Use a Grain Filler to Get a Deep, Lustrous Look

A grain filler is a crucial step to getting a professional-quality mirror finish. Though some woodworkers try to fill grain using a slurry of sanding dust and oil or multiple coats of finish, all that repeated finish application and sanding is laborious and time-consuming. A better option is to use a commercial oil- or water-based grain filler.

OIL-BASED FILLERS

Behlen Pore-O-Pac™ Grain Filler

Colors: Natural, medium walnut, mahogany
I used a paddle mixer to stir this filler to an even viscosity, then thinned it in the ratio of 3 parts filler to 1 part mineral spirits. It set up the fastest of the oil-based fillers, forcing me to work on a smaller area at a time, but the initial results were reasonably good.

Old Masters® Woodgrain Filler

Color: Natural (deep gray)
This product is easily mixed by hand. To add color, it is recommended to add "1 part stain to 2 parts filler" because it needs the binder in a stain to perform as required. It was easy to work because it didn't set up very quickly, but it had a gummy texture. The initial results were reasonably good.

WATER-BASED FILLERS

Aqua Coat® Wood Grain Filler

Color: Clear
This is an easy-to-use filler with low odor, but because it's a gel, removing the surplus was a bit difficult. Also, it takes a little more time to incorporate a color into the gel. It sands easily. Both this and the Crystalac can be used as clear fillers.

Crystalac® Wood Grain Filler

Color: Clear
This filler had low odor and dried slowly enough to make it easy to apply but fast enough to apply a second coat fairly quickly. It was easy to sand. If you want to color a filler, I'd give this a slight edge over the Aqua Coat because it was easier to incorporate color into it.

Behlen Water Base Grain Filler

Colors: Neutral, mahogany, brown
This product filled very well but dried extremely quickly, making it difficult to work. The surface had to be sanded to remove the final residue. I'd be cautious using this on veneered work. It's the only water-based filler used that is available in wood tones.

Check your progress. To tell if you've reached the right amount or saturation of color in the filler, wipe some on a white paper plate. You want it to be pretty opaque, as in the left-hand sample.

Consistent consistency. When you've achieved the right color, strain the filler through two layers of cheesecloth to remove lumps.

three sections with oil-based as opposed to six with a faster-drying, water-based type.

Some fillers come in wood tones, while others are only available as "neutral" or "natural." Unless you want gray pores, these clear fillers must be colored. For oil-based fillers, you can use any solvent-compatible colorants such as artist's oil paints, dry pigments, or universal tinting colors (UTCs). For water-based fillers, you can use Mixol® concentrates, UTCs, or artist's acrylics.

It is best to blend the color thoroughly with a small amount of filler and mineral spirits (or water for water-based fillers) and then add that to a batch of filler; it will incorporate much more easily than if you add the color directly to the batch. If you use dry pigments, mix them in well; otherwise, you may have a pocket of unmixed pigment smeared on the surface.

If a can of filler has been sitting on a shelf for a long time, you may find that the solids have become tightly packed at the bottom. Don't throw it away; it may be perfectly

viable. Use a metal paddle mixer chucked into a drill, or ask the local paint store to put it in a paint shaker. After you've added any necessary color, thin the filler to the consistency of medium cream.

Sand, stain, and seal the wood first

You need a grain filler only if you want a film finish on an open-pored wood, such as a period reproduction made from walnut or mahogany, or a contemporary piece made from any open-pored wood such as white oak or ash.

Prepare the surface as you normally would. Sand to 180- or 220-grit, and then apply dye or stain if desired. Next, instead of a full or heavy coat of clear finish, apply a thin washcoat. It seals the surface but does not distort or close off the top of the pores, which would interfere with filling them.

The washcoat should have a solids content of 7% to 15%. Two good options are a 1-lb. cut of dewaxed blond shellac, which has about 10% solids, or lightly thinned vinyl sealer, which has about 14% to 20%. I apply my washcoat with a French-polishing type of pad or even just an industrial paper towel folded flat. On a large top, the pad or towel should be wet but not soaking. Apply a thin, wet coat quickly and leave it alone. If you do need to sand, be very careful not to cut through the seal coat and especially your color coat. A safe way is to use the back of the sandpaper and do a light burnish.

Apply the filler, then remove the surplus

Apply the filler using a stiff-bristle brush. Brushes with short, thick bristles work best

A single coat. Wipe or brush on the thinned shellac. Resist the urge to touch up areas that absorb the finish. You are only sealing the wood, not finishing it.

Hide or Enhance the Grain?

You can emphasize the grain structure by making the filler slightly darker, a technique found on a lot of antiques (left section of panel). You can use a clear water-based filler to leave the wood looking unchanged, apart from the smooth finish (center). Finally, you can have the grain filler match the dyed or natural color of the finished wood to minimize the grain structure (right).

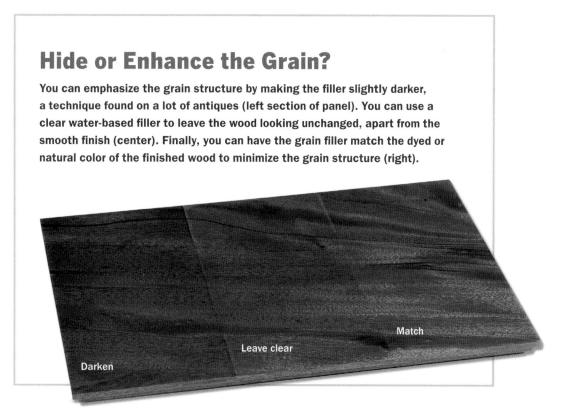

Darken

Leave clear

Match

Brush in the filler. Both types of filler are applied in the same way, either with a brush or rubbed into the grain with your hand. Because the water-based fillers dry faster than the oil-based ones, you should work a smaller area at a time. If you try to cover too large an area, the filler may harden before you can remove the surplus.

Hand applied. Gedrys likes to work the filler into the wood with the heel of his gloved hand.

at forcing the filler into the grain (see the photo at top). Be sure to clean the brush well afterward or it will harden like a rock. After applying the filler, wait a few minutes and then remove any excess using a plastic putty knife or scraper. The filler should roll up the blade. If you're pushing liquid across the surface, give the filler a little longer to set up. Scrape away the bulk of the surplus, wait a few more minutes (less for water-based

fillers), and then go over the surface with a white non-abrasive pad. Move the pad diagonally to the grain, first in one direction and then the opposite. Use a light touch so as not to remove any filler from the grain. Finally, go lightly with the grain to remove any remaining excess. The action is a lot like erasing chalk from a blackboard.

If you apply filler over too large an area and it is setting faster than you can remove it, wipe the surface with a cloth or paper towels wet with mineral spirits (or water for water-based fillers) and start over. This will only work if the filler hasn't fully hardened. If that happens, you will have to sand away the surplus and most likely dye and seal the surface again.

How to tell when you're done

Use a raking light to examine the surface. It should appear a little dull and have no visible removal marks. If you see crosshatching lines left by the putty knife or the pad, go over these lightly using the white pad with the grain. Don't worry if you still see a slight

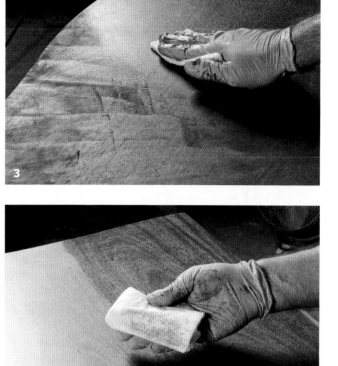

1. Not ready to remove. Don't try to squeegee away the surplus filler while it is still shiny and liquid. You'll just pull it out of the pores.

2. Work quickly. Move the squeegee at a 45° angle to the grain to scrape away the surplus but leave the grain filled. You have a narrow window from when the filler starts to set up to when it becomes too hard to work.

3. This beats burlap. To remove the residue missed by the squeegee, Gedrys uses a white, non-abrasive pad instead of the traditional burlap, which can scratch the wood.

4. A final wipe down. After an oil-based filler has cured for at least an hour, gently wipe the surface with a cloth dampened with mineral spirits to remove any haze of filler left on the surface.

Dealing with details. Once the pad becomes loaded with filler, you can use it to fill the grain on carved and curved areas (top). You don't want to leave surplus filler anywhere, so use a sharpened dowel to clean out recesses and corners (above).

trace of the pores; the finish will bridge this. If you need to fill the grain a second time, as I often do on woods with large, deep pores such as most mahoganies, wait 24 hours. Once the grain is filled and the surface is clean, let the filler rest for at least 48 hours and preferably three to four days to let all the solvents evaporate before applying a clear topcoat. If you don't, within six months there will be little bubbles in your finish. This is called "solvent pop," and the only way to fix it is to strip the finish and start over.

Apply the clear coat the same way as for unfilled wood with two precautions: Before using a water-based finish over an oil-based filler, or vice versa, first seal the filler with a 2-lb. cut of shellac. Before you use solvent lacquer, apply a coat of vinyl sealer over either type of filler.

All Finishes Have a Shelf Life

JEFF JEWITT

Few things are more annoying than opening a $30 quart of varnish you bought last year only to find the remaining two-thirds has solidified into a gel. It's an expensive reminder that tools may last a lifetime, but finishes don't.

All finishes have a shelf life, which is the amount of time that a product remains usable. I'll show you how to maximize the shelf life of finishing materials and, more importantly, how to tell when they've gone to the dark side.

Buy it fresh and date it

I'm as cheap as anybody, but when it comes to finishes, "buy more, save more" isn't a good strategy. Try to anticipate how much finish you'll use over the next year and don't buy more than that. Some manufacturers publish shelf-life figures and date products clearly, but many don't.

Always date your finish. On the container, write the date that you dissolved the shellac or mixed your own wiping varnish. After six months, test the finish before use, even if it looks fine. Also, label brand-new finish with the purchase date or the date provided by the manufacturer.

Keep the lid tight. If the inside of a lid has become encrusted with finish and won't fully screw on, soak it in lacquer thinner and then scrub it with steel wool.

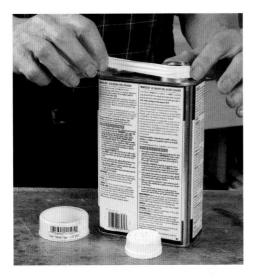

The self-draining trick. Use a nail to punch four or five holes in the rim of a standard container. When finish gets into the rim, it will drip back into the can.

Nonstick finish. Wrap a screw top with Teflon® plumber's tape. Finish won't stick to it, you'll get a much better seal, and the lid will screw on and off more easily.

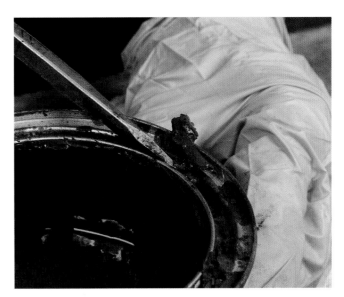

Clean the rim. Oil-based finishes start to harden when exposed to oxygen, so keep them in an airtight container. To maintain a good seal, dig out any dried finish that has collected in the rim, and wipe down the rim after each use.

Never buy cans with rusty lids, the ones you often see "on sale"—the condition of the can indicates poor storage or old age. Try to buy finishes like you buy milk: Look for a manufacturing date. If you don't understand the dating code, ask a clerk for help. If there is no date, write the date of purchase on the can. Label all your finishes, including those you've mixed yourself.

Store finish in a cool place, between 55°F and 70°F. Chemical reactions accelerate as the temperature rises, and almost all processes that cause finish to go bad involve chemical reactions. A cool basement is better than a hot garage. Most finishes are OK if stored below 55°, with the exception of waterborne. If you work in a cold shop, store your waterborne finishes in the house, and never let them freeze. Bring all finishes up to 55° to 70° before you use them. Also, keep the lid tight. If necessary, transfer the product to a container with a tighter lid.

Oil-Based

Oil-based finishes can last indefinitely, but only if you keep oxygen away.

Product	Shelf life before opening	Shelf life after opening	Brand names	Comments	Unusable when
Linseed oil (boiled and raw)	Indefinite	Indefinite	Klean-Strip®, Crown®, Sunnyside	Can be thinned with mineral spirits if necessary.	Will not strain, is thick and jelly-like
Tung oil	Indefinite	Indefinite	Hope's®, Master's Blend™, Rockler®, Woodcraft®	Can be thinned with mineral spirits if necessary.	Will not strain, is thick and jelly-like
Danish oil, oil and varnish blends	Indefinite	Indefinite if properly stored	Watco®, Deft®, General Finishes®	Pour into smaller containers or use Bloxygen®.	Hardened or jelly-like
Tung-oil-based varnish	Indefinite	Indefinite in ideal conditions; typically 3–4 years	Waterlox® and some spar varnishes	Shortest shelf life once opened. Pour into smaller containers or use Bloxygen.	Jelly-like consistency
Alkyd varnishes	Indefinite	Indefinite if properly stored	Pratt & Lambert® 38® Clear Varnish, Old Masters Super Varnish	Forms skin after prolonged oxygen exposure, but liquid underneath is generally usable.	Hardened or jelly-like
Oil-based polyurethane	Indefinite	Indefinite if properly stored	Minwax®, Deft, Varathane®, Cabot®, Behlen	Forms skin after prolonged oxygen exposure, but liquid underneath is generally usable.	Hardened or jelly-like

Keep oxygen out of oil-based finishes

Any finish based on a drying oil will harden when exposed to oxygen. These include tung and linseed oils, so-called Danish oils, and oil-based varnishes and polyurethanes. If you're not careful when storing these products, oxygen will cause them to harden prematurely.

When a can is full, there's no room for oxygen. But as you use the finish, you create "head space" as the can fills with air. Exposed to oxygen, the finish will gradually skin over, or the whole liquid may start to gel.

Kept in tightly sealed containers with minimal head space, raw or boiled linseed

Myth: Storing upside down prolongs shelf life. Storing a half-empty can of oil-based finish upside down does nothing to displace the air and will not prolong the life of the contents.

Good under the skin. If the finish only has a thin skin on it, the liquid underneath should still be usable. Pour it through a strainer into a new container.

Too far gone. If the oil-based finish has started to gel, or if you create lots of small flakes trying to break through the skin, it is probably not worth using.

oil and tung oil can last five or more years. It might thicken with age, but if it isn't cloudy and gummy, it should be usable. Danish oil-type products are mostly oil and solvent. They may thicken but are usable as long as they are clear and liquid.

On the other hand, when air gets into cans of oil-based varnish and polyurethane, one of two things will happen. In some products, a skin will form. If you can break the skin and get at the liquid, it's generally usable. But, in tung oil-based varnishes like Waterlox, air can gel the entire contents, rendering them unusable.

To minimize exposure to oxygen, transfer finish to smaller containers as you use it (I use glass Mason and baby food jars). Or, use a product like Bloxygen, which replaces the air with a heavier gas. To test the finish, pour it through a medium-mesh strainer (the cone-shaped type available at hardware and paint stores). If it strains, it's good.

Even flakes have a shelf life

When you dissolve dry shellac flakes in alcohol, the shelf-life clock starts ticking faster. This is due to esterification, a gradual chemical reaction between alcohols and organic acids (shellac is made up of organic acids). The reaction produces chemicals called esters, which are softer and tackier than the normally hard shellac resin. They are also more prone to water-spotting.

Less-refined shellac grades like button, seedlac, and waxy grades will esterify at a much slower rate and may last over a year once dissolved. Dewaxed, bleached grades such as super blond should be used within six months to a year, depending on the "cut," or the ratio of flakes to alcohol. That goes for all mixed shellac: the more alcohol, the shorter the shelf life.

Shellac

Shellac has a shelf life both as flakes and when dissolved. Old shellac will take longer to dry and won't create a durable finish.

Product	Shelf life before opening	Shelf life after opening	Brand names	Comments	Unusable when
Shellac flakes, waxy (includes seedlac and buttonlac, waxy orange and lemon)	5 or more years in cool, dry conditions	(After mixing) 1–2 years in cool, dry conditions	Woodcraft and various online retailers	When mixed, thinner cuts have shorter shelf life. Refrigerate unused flakes.	Mixed with alcohol, a jelly forms
Shellac flakes, dewaxed (includes super blond, blond, pale, etc.)	1–2 years in cool, dry conditions	(After mixing) 6–12 months in cool, dry conditions	Woodcraft and various online retailers	When mixed, thinner cuts have shorter shelf life. Refrigerate unused flakes.	Mixed with alcohol, a jelly forms
Shellac, premixed	3 years	3 years if properly stored	Zinsser® Bulls Eye®, SealCoat™	Zinsser dates all its products. Buy the freshest date.	Won't dry quickly or stays tacky

Flakes won't dissolve. If flakes don't dissolve, they're no good.

Liquid won't harden. To test the viability of old shellac, pour a small puddle onto an impermeable surface. If it's tacky after an hour, dispose of it.

Keep it cool. Refrigerating shellac flakes slows their deterioration.

Myth: Vacuum-packing extends shelf life. Vacuum-sealing a bag of flakes doesn't extend its shelf life. The chemical breakdown isn't affected by oxygen.

Myth: Grinding also extends shelf life. Turning old shellac flakes into powder may make them dissolve in alcohol, but it will still produce an inferior finish.

Fill to the brim. Fill a smaller jar with your oil-based finish from a partially used can. This will prolong the life of the leftover finish by minimizing its contact with oxygen.

Or replace the air. After using some of the contents, spray inert gas into the container to replace the air and prevent the remaining finish from hardening.

To test whether dissolved shellac is still viable, pour a drop onto an impermeable surface such as glass or laminate. If it's good, it will dry enough to be tack-free (your finger won't stick to it) within an hour.

Dry flakes also have a shelf life. Bleached and dewaxed flakes are the most prone to going bad, while unrefined waxy grades can last for years. In general, try to use flakes within a year after purchase.

There are a couple of myths about prolonging the shelf life of shellac. Some folks say that old shellac can be forced to dissolve by grinding it. Not true. Bad shellac is bad regardless of the size of the flakes.

The second myth is that vacuum-sealing shellac flakes makes them last longer. In fact, dry shellac reacts with itself over time, slowly becoming insoluble in alcohol. Heat accelerates the reaction, but oxygen has no effect. Probably, this myth persists because most folks vacuum-seal flakes and then refrigerate them, which will prolong their shelf life.

Waterborne finishes have different problems

It's hard to generalize shelf life and storage needs for waterborne finishes because there are so many types. In general, I try to use them within a year, two at the most. Keep cans tightly sealed in a cool, dry place, and don't let them freeze. Bad waterborne finish has a cheesy, curdled consistency, or it separates like oil and water, even after shaking. The additives in waterborne finishes can deactivate over time, causing them to "fisheye" or become foamy after they're applied. If a product is more than a year old, run it through a mesh filter and test it on a sample board before you use it. (If in doubt, throw it out.)

Waterborne gone bad. When a waterborne finish gets too old, it can curdle and get lumpy, like sour milk.

Head space doesn't cause problems with most waterborne finishes, but dried finish around the lid seal does. Again, transfer unused finish to a smaller container (glass or plastic) with a tight-fitting lid.

Long live lacquer

One of the few products with a long shelf life is plain old solvent-based furniture lacquer, also known as nitrocellulose lacquer. Because there are no reactive components in the resin, it should store for many years if you keep it close to the 55°F to 70°F range.

Waterborne

Use waterborne finishes within a year or two of purchase and store them at between 55°F and 70°F. If they freeze, throw them out.

Product	Shelf life before opening	Shelf life after opening	Brand names	Comments	Unusable when
Waterborne finishes	1–2 years	1–2 years if properly stored	General Finishes, Varathane, Behlen, Target, Minwax, Deft	Don't use waterborne finishes older than 2 years.	Discolored, lumpy, or rubbery when strained; test with strainer

Lacquer

Furniture lacquer is among the longest-lasting clear finishes. It can stay usable for many years when stored correctly.

Product	Shelf life before opening	Shelf life after opening	Brand names	Comments	Unusable when
Nitro-cellulose lacquer	Indefinite	Indefinite	Deft Clear Wood Finish, Minwax	Store in original container with tight seal.	Severely discolored, cloudy, or rubbery sediment

Old lacquer can be thinned. Solvent-based lacquer may thicken with age, but a dash of thinner can bring it back to life.

Dyes and Stains

Concentrated dyes, whether liquid or powder, and pigment stains can last for decades in their premixed form.

Product	Shelf life before opening	Shelf life after opening	Brand names	Comments	Unusable when
Oil-based pigment wiping stains	Indefinite	Indefinite if stored in an airtight container	Minwax, General Finishes	If skin develops, product underneath should be usable.	Hardened
Dye powders and concentrates unmixed	Indefinite	Indefinite	J.E. Moser's, Lockwood, Homestead, Arti	Can last 20 years or more.	Doesn't dissolve in solvent
Dyes, premixed with water or solvents	Indefinite	Indefinite	Behlen Solar-Lux™, General Finishes	Never store dyes in metal containers. Use plastic or glass.	Severe color change from original; doesn't dissolve in solvent

Oxygen has no effect on lacquer. It may thicken if the solvent evaporates, but just add lacquer thinner and keep the lid tight. I've seen lacquers yellow in the can over time, but this generally doesn't affect appearance.

Stains and dyes last long

Pigment stains are forgiving when it comes to shelf life and storage. They should store just fine for years. (Oil-based gel stains are an exception; treat them like other oil-based finishes.) One caution: Don't let waterborne stains freeze, or they'll become "cheesy" or curdled.

Concentrated liquid or powdered dyes have a virtually infinite shelf life. Try to use mixed dyes within a year, but as long as you store them in a metal-free container to avoid rust, they can last much longer. Always test older pigments and dyes on a scrap to confirm the color hasn't changed.

Dye another day. Water-based dyes, once dissolved, will last a year or more if kept in a non-metallic container.

Brushes for Woodworkers

PETER GEDRYS

Visit a pro finisher's shop and you are likely to be confronted with a bewildering array of brushes: round handles, flat handles, bristles long and short, ox hair, goat hair, squirrel hair, and nylon. Why do I have so many? The most important thing that a finisher knows about brushes is exactly what a woodworker knows about router bits: One size and shape does not fit all.

That's because there's more to finishing than just brushing liquid onto flat, rectangular surfaces. The brush that works well for that isn't the best choice for narrow or curved surfaces.

To help you pick the right one, here's an overview of the brushes that I use most often. With a little guidance, you can put together a custom brush kit that will help you handle any situation, from applying clear finishes on flat surfaces to detail work with dyes and glazes.

Foam is surprisingly good

Dip and tip. To avoid bubbles in the finish, don't press the sponge against the cup. Instead, angle it upward to let the liquid soak in (inset). Foam leaves a smooth finish with no brush marks (right).

Clear winners for clear finishes

A good finish brush should hold a generous amount of liquid, releasing it only at the point of contact with the surface. There are some general rules to follow: use synthetic filaments for waterborne finishes, and natural filaments for solvent-based finishes.

Flat surfaces

For finishing large, flat surfaces like doors or tabletops with varnish or waterborne products, a foam brush is my first choice.

Why? The biggest reason is that a foam brush lays down an even coat of finish with no brush marks. Contrary to popular myth, a foam brush won't leave bubbles in your finish. Just be sure to steer clear of the super-cheap ones with minimal interior support. Look for the ones that have a plastic support right up to the bevel.

Go wide. Gedrys favors an extrawide, short-bristle brush for applying shellac over large areas. The extra width minimizes the overlapping strokes that can create unsightly lines in your finish.

Natural china hog bristles for shellac

For small, flat surfaces. This brush is great for narrow, flat surfaces. Gedrys puts the brush inside a disposable glove (inset) to keep it from drying out between coats.

Ox hair

Goat hair dome mop

Also, take care in loading the brush. First, dampen it on the bevel and just above it with a few drops of the appropriate solvent, then dip it into the finish just past the bevel. Take the brush out of the finish and turn the bevel faceup to let the liquid soak in. Repeat this dip and turn once more for a useful charge of finish.

Foam brushes are terrific, but I avoid using them with shellac because the alcohol in the shellac will melt the foam. So, for applying shellac on large, flat surfaces, I use an extrawide brush (see the bottom right photo on the facing page) made with ordinary natural white china hog bristles. This brush is 4 in. wide with short (1¾-in.) bristles (varnish and gesso brush No. 85062100; www. kremerpigments.com). The generous width lets me cover a lot of surface area quickly without frequent reloading.

Details

For profiled surfaces and other details, I use a flat brush with short 1-in. filaments. The one shown above is made with soft ox hair (Habico No. 660D; Sepp Leaf Products, 800-971-7377). The brush is small,

measuring just 6 in. long. The handle is flat and extremely thin, making it comfortable to hold and easy to control. The filaments are beveled at the tip and lay down a very fine coat due to the softness of the hair.

This little brush can cover a lot of ground. Once the brush is fully charged with varnish, I can easily do the narrow facets of the raised panels of a large door and I only have to dip it in the finish once or twice.

For applying clear finish to irregular surfaces, my first choice is a round brush shaped like a mop (shown at right) and made

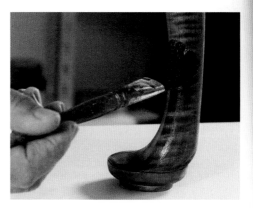

Curved surfaces. For curved areas, the shape and softness of this mop brush allow it to apply finish evenly.

WINSOR & NEWTON SERIES 140 ENGLAND

3/4

Stay Synthetic for Waterborne

To apply waterborne finishes on flat surfaces, Gedrys uses foam brushes again. But for irregular surfaces and details, he chooses mops and flat brushes with nylon bristles.

Nylon bristle filbert

Foam

with very soft goat hair (Winsor & Newton 140 series wash, ¾ in. or ⅞ in.; www.winsornewton.com).

The brush holds a lot of finish. Fully loaded, it can lay a thin, even coat on a table leg without reloading. The soft hairs are also long and flexible enough that they can lie flat and conform to any surface you're finishing—a huge help on parts like turned table legs, especially those that are tapered or reeded.

Despite its softness, the brush holds a great "point," coming to a well-defined narrow tip that is ideal for finishing carved details such as ball-and-claw feet.

Best brushes for color

I use a different set of small artist's brushes for tasks like isolating veneers, cutting in dyes, blending glazes, and touch-ups.

Small brushes for small details

For detail work that calls for fine lines of color, I use small, round artist's brushes in several sizes (Winsor & Newton series 101, sizes 1 to 3; www.winsornewton.com). A good round brush is made with a mix of natural sable and synthetic filaments. The brush holds a sharp point—ideal for tasks like applying narrow lines of shellac over holly stringing, to keep it lighter than the surrounding surface after stain is applied. I also use rounds to hide filler for nail or screw holes, adding fine lines of color to mimic the grain. I also have several flat artist's brushes in sizes ranging from 10mm to 19mm (Winsor & Newton Series 606; www.winsornewton.com). These lay down a very straight line; I use them when blending sapwood to heartwood or adding dye adjacent to stringing that I've already isolated.

Small round artist

Flat artist

Master the fine points. Small round artist's brushes are ideal for touching up damaged finishes and other fine detail work.

Flat and straight. The rectangular shape of this brush helps it follow a line—even a curved one—very accurately.

Two specialists for glazing

When working with glazes, I keep two brushes handy: one for applying glaze to detail areas and another for blending glaze across a larger surface. These two brushes are as different as night and day. One has a limited row of stiff hair shaped like a fan and the other has long, soft, squared-off bristles.

A fan brush, used with a pushing or pouncing motion, is great for applying small amounts of glaze to detail areas like cock beading or reeded legs (Cambridge fan, size 4; www.winsornewton.com). Fans can

Every finisher needs a fan. The broom-like bristles of this brush are used to pounce and daub glaze into hard-to-reach areas.

Fan

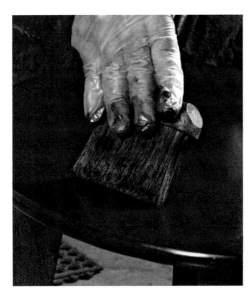

A brush for blending. The softener removes excess color and blends what remains. Wipe the excess glaze onto a paper towel dampened with solvent.

Non-ferrule softener

be purchased with hairs of different tensile strengths—stiffer for pushing glaze into recesses and softer for blending.

To blend out and feather glaze on a larger scale, I use a softener (Cadet hog softener, 100mm). Whisk the brush lightly and consistently across a surface to eliminate any application lines.

Sanding Basics

JEFF JEWITT

Even if the wood's surface appears perfect after you've run it through the tablesaw, jointer, or planer, it's not. All of these machines leave their marks, and the tricky part is that those marks often aren't visible on bare wood. Unfortunately, they'll jump out once a stain or clear finish is applied. That's why all boards coming off a machine need further leveling and smoothing.

The type of preparation you use—hand, machine, or a mix of the two—will be dictated partly by the piece you're working on. If you're making a period reproduction where nuanced tool marks are a sign of handcraftsmanship, all you may need is a final quick sanding with very fine sandpaper after using scrapers and planes. However, most woodworkers want a dead-flat and smooth surface, and the way to achieve this is with modern abrasives and sanding machines. Here I'll give you my time-tested methods for getting the best results with these tools.

The big challenge: flattening wide panels

I've been answering woodworking and finishing questions for more than 20 years and one thing that causes a lot of head-scratching is how to flatten a multi-board panel. It is too wide to go through your planer, your handplane skills may not be up to the challenge, and your 5-in. random-orbit

Start with power. To smooth a panel efficiently, combine machine and hand techniques, working from coarser to finer-grit abrasives. First, use a 5-in. or 6-in. random-orbit sander, starting with 150-grit paper and finishing with 180-grit. Jewitt uses cushioned work gloves to dampen the sander's vibration.

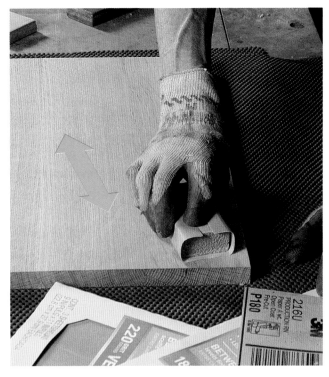

Hand-sanding disks. If you find it tiring to grip a sanding block for long periods, use a strap-on hand pad designed for hook-and-loop disks.

Finish by hand. After power-sanding to 180-grit, Jewitt starts hand-sanding with 220-grit paper wrapped around a cork sanding block. Your shop teacher may have yelled at you if you didn't sand with the grain, but sanding at a slight bias of 7° to 10° shears off the wood fibers better without leaving visible cross-grain scratches.

End with the end grain. You can usually stop sanding face grain at 220-grit, but go to 400-grit on end grain for a glass-smooth finish.

sander is inadequate. To cap it all off, this panel often becomes the most visible part of a project, whether it is a tabletop, a desktop, or the sides or top of a chest of drawers. It needs to be perfect.

My answer is to use a belt sander. But the first step in my flattening process occurs during glue-up, when I align the boards as carefully as possible. I clamp 1½-in.-square battens across the glue-up near the ends and in the middle to sandwich the boards into alignment. I use laminate-faced battens to repel glue, but packing tape will work, too. I then partially tighten the bar clamps underneath the board and try to bring the joints flush where there's any misalignment, using a non-marking mallet for extra persuasion. When the panel is as flush as possible, I apply the rest of the bar clamps and snug them all down.

Despite these precautions, unless you're very lucky, there will still be some bumps at the joints. This is where you bring in the heavy equipment. The best tool for the job is a large 4-in. by 24-in. belt sander. A second choice, though slower, is a good-quality 6-in. random-orbit sander with either a barrel grip or a pistol grip.

When sanding panels, you level the surface by bringing the high spots down to the low ones, removing the milling marks at the same time. To do this logically and efficiently, I use a crosshatch technique just the way you would when using a scrub plane to level large panels. While it's counterintuitive because most have been taught to sand "with the grain," this technique levels better. Start by drawing some pencil or chalk lines across the width of the panel. Load the sander with 100- or 120-grit paper and move it across the panel at a 45° angle. Make three to five passes down the whole panel, overlapping strokes by an inch or two, then switch to the opposing 45° angle and do the same. Keep

Clamp down, then across.
A flat glue-up speeds sanding. First clamp the boards between battens to bring them flush. Then apply pressure across the panel to make the joints tight (above). To prevent gumming up the sandpaper, scrape off dried glue (right) before you start sanding.

Flatten a large panel. Panels that are too wide for a jointer and planer, like a glued-up tabletop, must be flattened before smoothing. A belt sander is the best power tool for the job.

switching until the lines are gone. Then sand the whole panel with strokes along the grain. As you work, check your progress with a straightedge. Once the surface is flat, you can start the smoothing process.

Attack from different directions for even stock removal. The best way to level joints between boards is to run the sander at 45° to the grain, first to the left (top) and then to the right (above).

Now go with the grain. Once the joints are level, sand with the grain to flatten the whole board.

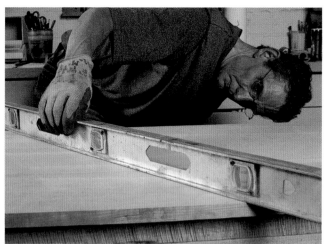

Check your progress. Use a straightedge that exceeds the width of the panel so that you can check for high spots. Once the panel is flat, you can start the smoothing process.

Smoothing flat surfaces by machine and by hand

Now switch to a 5-in. or 6-in. random-orbit sander and continue smoothing the surface with 150-grit disks, then 180-grit disks. This time, move the sander with the grain or at a slight angle. With random-orbit sanding, you should not skip grits. One reason these machines sand more efficiently is because they put cross-grain scratches in the wood. If you skip grits, more than likely you'll see coarse scratch marks later.

One of the hardest things is to know when you've sanded enough with a particular grit. Trust your eyes and your hands. Work at a comfortable height and with a strong light source on the far side of the workpiece. If you don't have a source of good natural backlighting, use a spotlight that you can position to rake the workpiece. As you sand, inspect the sandpaper periodically to make sure it's not clogging up or wearing out. Power sanders that have dust extraction are a must in today's shop, but the disks will eventually wear out, so examine the edges for worn grit, tears, or creases. Don't be frugal—worn-out sandpaper can do more harm than good.

Narrow parts. On a narrow surface, it is easy to tip the sander to one side, rounding over the crisp edge (left). Sanding multiple narrow sections at once not only creates a stable surface to sand on but also speeds up the process (below).

Tight corners. To reach right into a corner without sanding across the grain, attach pressure-sensitive adhesive (PSA) sandpaper to a small block, or mount regular paper to the block using spray adhesive.

Keep your sandpaper clean. When hand- or machine-sanding, the sandpaper can get clogged with dust (1). To clean it, swipe the sandpaper across a piece of synthetic abrasive pad (2). The result is clean sandpaper that keeps cutting longer (3).

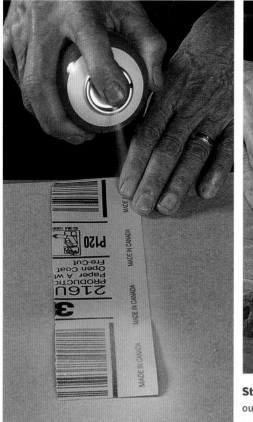

Stick it and sand it. For shallow curves, make a flexible sanding block out of a ⅛-in.-thick strip of wood. Attach the sandpaper to it using spray-mount adhesive (left), or use pressure sensitive adhesive (PSA) paper.

Your flexible friend. This thin rubber sanding block can be flexed to match a variety of contours.

Match the profile. You can buy rubber shapes like this teardrop sander that match common convex and concave profiles, or look around your shop for suitable alternatives such as dowels.

Once you have power-sanded to at least 180-grit, you are ready to sand by hand. Tear a sheet of sandpaper into the size you want, typically quarters. I have an old hacksaw blade mounted on the edge of my workbench to do this. Back up the sandpaper with a sanding block. You can also use hook-and-loop disk sandpaper with a grip-faced hand pad. Hand-sanding is rough on the hands, so wear garden gloves or work gloves. I buy the ones with rubberized palms so I can get a better grip on the sandpaper and the part I'm working on.

Every woodworker is taught to hand-sand by pushing the paper with the grain. However, I prefer to hand-sand at a slight bias of 7° to 10° because it slices off wood fibers better. If you've done a good job sanding on the machine, you can probably begin and end the hand-sanding using 220-grit paper.

Because hand-sanding always leaves a scratch pattern that follows the grain or blends in with it, you can get away with skipping grits. For example, you can start hand-sanding at 100-grit, go to 150, and then skip to 220. If you're just starting out as a woodworker and are not yet sure of your technique, play it safe and don't skip grits.

How to handle curved surfaces—

On complicated areas such as moldings, carvings, routed profiles, and rounded or curved areas, a power sander can ruin the shape, so you must sand by hand. When you hand-sand curved surfaces, always try to back up the sandpaper with a rigid or semi-rigid block that matches the wood's profile. The woodworking and automotive industries both offer flexible sanding blocks designed for contour sanding. You also could use dowels or custom blocks made from rigid foam insulation. On more intricate profiles, just use your fingers or hand.

When to stop sanding

How far you sand is a question that's been argued and debated by woodworkers for decades. In most cases, you shouldn't have to sand past 220-grit; however, some woods reveal greater luster and figure if you sand with finer grits. In these cases, you be the judge: Look at finished samples side by side that have been sanded to different grits to see if the extra work pays off.

There are times when sanding to a higher grit definitely makes a difference. The first is when using water-based finish, where you get a lot of grain-raising when you apply the first coat or two. Sanding to 320- or 400-grit will leave smaller "shards" of torn cellular material, which leads to less raised grain. Another example is sanding end grain: Going up to 320- or 400-grit leaves a more uniform finished appearance.

Always check your sanding before you apply a stain or finish. Examine the surface in raking light and then wipe down the wood with mineral spirits, denatured alcohol, or water (see the photos on p. 46). Use one of the latter two if you're using a water-based finish, but if you use water you will have to smooth away the raised grain with the last grit you used. As well as wiping away sanding "swarf" (the mix of sawdust and worn-off sandpaper grit), the liquid will highlight any low spots, milling marks, and sanding scratches.

Once the wood feels dry to the touch, you can correct any problems by sanding again with 150-grit or 180-grit paper, then progress to 220 (or the highest grit you used in that area). Try not to work a small area too much or you'll risk creating a depression that will show when finish is applied. Rather, sand away the blemish and then gradually feather outward to blend in the repair. Sanding is a lot of work, but remember, the foundation of any fine finish is a well-sanded surface.

Raking light reveals hills and hollows. Shine a low light along the panel to make sure it is dead flat.

Wet the wood. Use denatured alcohol, mineral spirits, or water to wet the wood and reveal any remaining sanding scratches or machine marks from the jointer or planer.

Are You Sanding Right?

TERI MASASCHI

Just about every woodworker has a random-orbit sander. They're cheap to buy, they can handle any job, and you don't need to serve an apprenticeship to use one effectively. But you do need to understand how the tool works. Most people don't. Perhaps they saw one being used on TV, a friend gave them a one-minute lesson, or more likely they simply slapped a disk on their new sander and hit the wood.

The result is too many pieces that show the telltale evidence of poor sanding. These include failure to remove planer and jointer marks or scratches from coarse sandpaper, and surfaces that are smooth but not flat, with depressions and rounded-over edges.

I'll tell you how to handle the sander correctly, what grits to start and end with, and how to check your progress. It's worth learning how to sand correctly, as sanding is the most critical part of the finishing process. A well-sanded piece is already half finished!

A light touch and a slow hand

One of the biggest sanding debates is about whether to land the sander on the surface running at full speed, to place it on the wood and then turn it on, or to try a compromise, touching down while the motor is still picking up speed. In truth, do whatever feels best (this can vary by model); it really doesn't matter. What is more important is how you sand once you begin.

Choose Your Weapon

The 5-in. sander is the one most woodworkers should buy first. It's versatile and a must for narrow surfaces such as chair legs, but there are some good reasons a 6-in. machine should be second on your list. If you do a lot of sanding, take a look at the Mirka® Ceros sander. It has the light weight and low center of gravity of an air sander, yet it is electric, so there's no need for a large compressor.

That said, the Ceros costs considerably more than most electric sanders.

Years ago, pressure-sensitive adhesive (PSA) disks were cheaper than hook-and-loop (H&L) ones, but if you were sanding a small piece you often had to discard a PSA disk before it was used up, whereas H&L disks can be reused. Now the cost has nearly evened out and most sanders come with a H&L pad. Yours should, too.

Don't spend extra on a sander with speed control: I have never understood why anyone would sand at lower speeds and not keep the sander at its maximum setting. The only exception is wet sanding or polishing, which you shouldn't do with an electric sander anyway because of the risk of shock.

Air power for hard-core sanders. The majority of professional finishers and large cabinet shops use air-powered sanders for several reasons: They are more compact, lighter, and less top-heavy than their electric counterparts. They have fewer moving parts, last longer, and can be repaired rather than being generally disposable. However, these sanders are air hogs and at 90 psi, they need 20 plus cubic feet of air per minute, which translates into a 50- or 60-gal. compressor, compressed air lines, and in-line air filters and driers. That is the real expense of these machines, which makes them hard to justify for a hobbyist.

5-in. sander is nimble. Almost everyone owns a 5-in.-dia. random-orbit sander. They aren't expensive, and they can handle almost any task from sanding chair legs and frame-and-panel assemblies to smoothing big tabletops.

6-in. sander covers more ground. The extra inch gives you nearly 45% more sanding surface, which not only covers large, flat surfaces faster but also does a better job of flattening them.

A key factor is how fast you move the sander over the workpiece. Some people work in a frenzy, moving the sander rapidly back and forth as if they were using a sanding block. Others spend too long sanding the same spot. The correct speed is 8 to 10 seconds per foot. The frenzied among you will find slowing down like coming off the highway and going 25 miles an hour, but skittering the tool around doesn't help: You can't possibly move faster than the sander's vibration. On the other hand, slowing down allows you to keep better track of your sanding pattern and to be sure you are covering the surface evenly.

Random-orbit sanders need to float on the surface with light pressure to produce an optimum orbital pattern. Don't push down on the sander in the belief that it will cut faster. You'll just cause the tool to bog down, load up the paper with dust, and leave swirl marks on the wood. Bearing down also will create excessive heat, which can warp the sander's pad. If the sandpaper is constantly wearing out only around the perimeter, the pad has been distorted by heat buildup around the edge and you need to replace it.

Other secrets of success

When sanding a wider surface, overlap each pass by between a third and a half to ensure even coverage. As for the edge of the workpiece, it's fine to overhang it slightly, but keep at least two-thirds of the pad on the surface to avoid the risk of tipping the sander and rounding over the edge. If you are working on narrow surfaces such as legs or the edges of boards that individually can't meet the two-thirds rule, consider clamping identical pieces together and sanding them collectively. The wider surface provides a more stable platform for the sander.

One thing you should never try to do with a sander is to break or bevel an edge. The

Slow and steady. Advance the sander at a rate of about 8 to 10 seconds per foot, rather than rushing the sander all over the place. This lets the sander do the work and lets you keep track of your pattern, so you sand uniformly.

Sand first, glue later. It is much easier to sand components before you glue them together.

If you must sand after assembly. If you glued parts together before sanding them, it can be difficult to sand corners without damaging adjacent parts. A large drywall-taping knife lets you work into the corner safely.

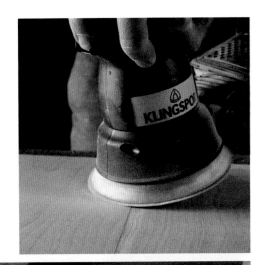

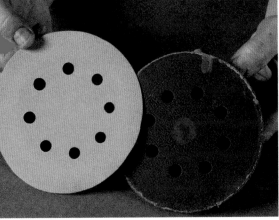

No tipping please. Don't try to concentrate the sanding power in a small area by tipping the sander (top). You'll create hollows in the surface. You also risk overheating the rim of the pad, causing it to expand. A sign this has happened is if the disk wears only toward the outside (above).

Manage the dust and grit. As well as keeping your lungs cleaner, attaching a vacuum lets sanders cut faster and extends the disk's lifespan.

Clean between grits. Remove any dust left on the workpiece before switching to a higher grit. It reduces the risk of coarse abrasive contaminating the finer disk, and it keeps the shop cleaner.

action is not designed to work on a narrow edge and you'll end up with an irregular surface. Break edges using a sanding block or bevel them with a block plane or a router bit.

There is no doubt that random-orbit sanders create enormous amounts of dust. Effective dust pickup from the sander will not only keep the air clear but also keep dust from packing the spaces between the abrasive particles and killing sanding efficiency. Hooking up a vacuum to the sander speeds stock removal and will extend the life of the disk.

Even with a vacuum attached, it is still necessary to sweep, vacuum, or blow off the surface before switching sandpaper to the next higher grit. Otherwise, leftover abrasive from the previous grit can create occasional deeper scratches even after you've switched to a finer disk.

1. It all comes together on tabletops. The tops of cabinets, chests, and tables are the most visible surfaces and therefore require the most careful sanding. The first stage is leveling the surface. The grit you choose depends on how much material you need to remove. Letting up to a third of the sander's pad overhang the edge of a work surface helps ensure uniform sanding. But go beyond a third and you risk tipping the sander and rounding the edge.

4. Then smooth. After you've removed surface imperfections with a coarse grit, the role of subsequent finer grits is to refine the scratch pattern. Here's a great way to know when to switch grits. Draw a light pencil line across the surface and sand the whole surface until the line is gone. Repeat and then move on to the next-grit disk.

2, 3. Check the surface. Looking across the surface into a raking light (above) helps reveal any imperfections. This pigtail squiggle (right) was probably caused by a piece of debris that the sander picked up when it was set down on the bench.

5. Hand-sand last. Once you've completed the final grit with the sander, use a sanding block with the same size grit, sanding with the grain. This removes any swirls left by the sander. Finally, use 180- or 220-grit paper and a sanding block to break the edges. Don't attempt this with a sander.

How to handle a frame-and-panel. Right and wrong sanding both before and after glue-up can make or break your frame-and-panel assemblies. Start with the flat surfaces first. It is fine to use a power sander on the raised portion of the panel and its back.

Hand-sand the profile. Don't use the sander, even on a flat, bevel-edged profile. Instead, hand-sand up to the same final grit as used on the sander. Go to 320- or 400-grit on the end-grain sections so they don't absorb too much finish and end up darker than their surroundings.

Guide to the grits, from start to finish

The first grit is unique: Its job is to remove surface defects. How coarse that grit should be depends on the severity of those defects: For large changes in height such as planer snipe or uneven edge-glued boards, you should start with 80- or 100-grit (it would be quicker, though, to remove the bulk of the high areas with either a handplane or a belt sander with a 100-grit belt). If the surface is essentially level but there is some tearout, you can start with 120-grit. If you have a smooth, flat surface left by either a well-tuned planer or handplane, you can start with 150-grit.

Stick with this first grit until all of the defects have been removed, and if it is taking too long, switch to a rougher grit. The purpose of subsequent higher grits is only to refine the scratch pattern of the previous grit, not to remove defects. If you switch to a higher grit when most of the defects are removed, you may never get rid of them. Most likely you will go through several disks

of this initial grit, so don't be tempted to extend their life. Most disks lose their cutting action dramatically after 15 to 40 minutes for coarse 80- to 120-grit disks and half that time for finer 180- to 220-grit disks. After that, it is time to toss them. Continuing to use these disks can cause the dreaded swirl or "pigtail" marks from sandpaper that is clogged. Second, don't think that if you start with 100-grit and use it long enough, it becomes 120- or 150-grit. It just creates 100-grit scratches, more and more slowly.

To see if you've removed all the defects, vacuum the dust, wipe on some denatured alcohol or mineral spirits, and check the surface with a raking light.

The two-line trick—The subsequent grits go much quicker. Draw a light pencil squiggle across the surface and sand the entire surface until it is gone. Draw a second line and sand it off. Now switch to the next-higher grit; it's as simple as that. As you move to higher grits—120, 150, 180, 220—the

Gang up parts. To sand the narrow sides of the frame, clamp them in pairs to provide a wider surface for the sander to ride on.

appearance of the surface will improve as coarse scratches are replaced by finer ones.

The industry standard for what should be the final grit is 220 for softwoods and 180 for hardwoods. This standard applies when using any film-building finish such as shellac, lacquer, and water- or oil-based polyurethane or varnish. But if the surface is going to get a French polish or a thin-finish such as a penetrating oil, then it is a good idea to continue up to 400-grit. If you can't find 320- or 400-grit disks locally, you can mail-order them or, if you have a small project, you can apply these grits by hand using sheets of sandpaper and a sanding block.

In any case, always do the final sanding by hand. Use the last grit that you used on the machine, wrap it around a cork-faced block or any firm sanding block, and sand with the grain in long, straight strokes. This will remove any sneaky swirl marks or other flaws and will soften the edges and refine delicate details. Check the surface again as before.

Sand the face after glue-up. After the frame is glued up, you need to level the joints. You may want to reduce major high spots with a handplane, but a random-orbit sander is ideal as it won't leave any cross-grain marks on adjacent parts.

You'll spot any flaws before you apply a clear coat or stain, and you can finish your project confident in its final appearance.

If you've never experienced a well-sanded project, you'll be surprised at how nicely the finish goes on.

Sandpaper: A Closer Look

TERI MASASCHI

When sanding is mentioned, most woodworkers groan. But sandpaper achieves results that no other tool can match. Whether it is taming wild grain without tearout, perfecting a curve, or getting a totally smooth surface prior to finishing, you'd be lost without sandpaper. And so would generations of woodworkers.

I'll show you how today's sandpaper can trace its ancestry back 800 years, tell you why different types of abrasives work best on different surfaces, and give you a tour of a sandpaper factory. I'll never convince you to like sanding, but you will gain a new respect for this disposable yet indispensable tool.

Modern abrasives go back a century

In 1891, a scientist trying to make synthetic diamonds invented silicon carbide, and a few years later, aluminum oxide, today's other main abrasive grit, was invented. The growth in automobile manufacturing, with all those shiny painted surfaces, increased demand for sandpaper, but only dry-sanding could be done as the hide glue used to bind the abrasive to the backing was not water resistant. In 1921, 3M invented the first waterproof paper and cut down on the problem of dust in factories.

Sand, Shells, and Sharks

As far back as the 13th century, the Chinese made sandpaper using a variety of abrasives such as sand and crushed shells, glued to parchment with a natural gum. Later, sharkskin was used as a fine abrasive. (The TV series *MythBusters* tested this story and found that sharkskin does indeed work as sandpaper with an abrasive equivalent to between 600- and 800-grit.) By the early 1800s, glass paper was being mass-produced; however, it dulled quickly because it was neither sharp enough nor hard enough.

Adhesives have continued to improve, and modern sanding products including sheets, disks, and belts use urea-formaldehyde and phenolic-resin glues. These are not only far more durable but also can withstand the heat generated by machine-sanding. However, you may still find a few sheets of sandpaper, particularly garnet, that are made with hide glue. Hold the paper close to your mouth and exhale on it. If it is hide glue, you'll get a whiff of that distinctive animal smell.

Parchment is no longer used as a backing, but paper still is. It is mostly used for hand-sanding but today's sheets can be treated for better water resistance and more flexibility.

Cloth backing is used for sanding products that need to be more durable but less flexible. Sanding belts are mostly cloth backed, as are disks for heavy, aggressive cutting. The cloth is cotton or polyester/cotton blends.

The right abrasive for the job

The manufacturing of abrasive grains is a science in itself. One crucial step common to all types of abrasive is a very precise process for separating the different-size particles. The heavier grits are sifted through screens, while the smaller, lighter grains are separated with air in a centrifugal system or by settling out in water.

Be aware that there are two standards for measuring particle size. The vast majority of papers now use the Federation of European Producers of Abrasives (FEPA) scale. FEPA products mostly have a "P" before the grit number. The United Abrasive Manufacturers Association (UAMA) is the successor to the Coated Abrasive Manufacturer's Institute (CAMI). Their scale, based on the American National Standards Institute (ANSI),

Aluminum oxide. Whether for power- or hand-sanding, the vast majority of abrasives used on bare wood are aluminum oxide.

Like broken tempered glass. Grains of aluminum oxide are rather like chunks of broken tempered glass—sharp but not pointy. But they break down easier than silicon carbide and therefore stay sharp longer on bare wood.

Silicon carbide. When sanding between coats or rubbing out the final finish, wet-sanding with silicon-carbide paper is the rule.

Like shards of regular glass. Grains of silicon carbide are pointier, rather like broken window glass. They require a hard surface such as a finish to break down and expose a sharp edge.

used to dominate domestic production but is now mostly confined to finer-grit wet-or-dry papers.

Up to 180-grit the two scales are very similar, but above that number the FEPA papers become increasingly coarser than ANSI-graded paper with the same number.

If you are uncertain which papers are which grades, stick to one brand.

Aluminum oxide vs. silicon carbide

In the last few years, new abrasives have entered the woodworking market (more

Super-hard new abrasives. Alumina zirconia and ceramic aluminum oxide are mostly used on sanding belts for fast stock removal. They also can be blended with aluminum oxide on disks.

also known as carborundum, is a compound of silicon and carbon. It is naturally dark gray but it has become an industry standard to attach it to the backer using a black resin, giving the sheets and disks a flat, black look.

Industry experts describe aluminum oxide as tough and blocky, while silicon carbide is sharper and pointier. Think of aluminum oxide as being like lumps of broken tempered glass, while silicon carbide is more like the shards from regular glass.

Both abrasives are "friable," meaning that in use the grains break up and expose fresh, sharp edges as opposed to staying whole and rapidly becoming blunt. But silicon carbide needs a harder surface than most woods to cause it to fracture and expose sharp surfaces. This makes aluminum oxide best on bare wood because by breaking down more, it lasts longer.

Conversely, when sanding between finishes, fine-grit silicon carbide has the sharpness to cut through the hardest finish, while aluminum oxide's blocky texture tends to glaze the surface. Using water or mineral spirits with wet-or-dry silicon-carbide paper prevents the paper from clogging, reduces heat that might damage the finish,

on those shortly), but aluminum oxide and silicon carbide remain dominant. While both are hard abrasives, their molecular structure makes them more complementary than competitive.

Aluminum oxide begins life as bauxite, also the raw material for aluminum. It comes in a range of colors from white to dark brown, but quite often the color is obscured by an adhesive tinted to designate whether the grit is coarse, fine, etc. Silicon carbide,

Garnet Is Yesterday's News

Garnet has a long history in woodworking and retains a loyal, though declining, number of fans. It is a natural mineral that, compared to aluminum oxide or silicon carbide, is relatively soft and fast-wearing. Industry insiders concede that it produces a very even scratch pattern on bare wood but no better than the latest grades of aluminum oxide. Any money you save buying garnet paper is probably more than offset by its faster wear.

eliminates dust, and creates a slurry. This mixture of liquid, abrasive particles, and finish can create a softer scratch pattern than if the paper is used dry.

Two tough new arrivals

Alumina zirconia is a synthetic blend of aluminum oxide and zirconium oxide. Hard, tough, and aggressive, it cuts almost as fast as silicon carbide but is less pointy. Typically found in coarser grits on sanding belts and disks, it is a good choice for fast stock removal on hardwood.

Harder still, ceramic aluminum oxide is made in a similar way to porcelain. It begins as a paste that is fired in a kiln and is then crushed into abrasive particles. Norton uses ceramic alumina on its 3X disks, while 3M uses it on its top-of-the-line products, which are mostly colored purple. If you have a lot of sanding to do and don't want to spend more time than you have to, it is probably worth the extra money to buy this type of abrasive.

1. PREP THE PAPER
Start with a blank roll. Sheets, disks, or belts all begin life as a large roll of backing material. The first step is to print on the back what the product will be.

How It's Made

Ali Industries, maker of the Gator® and Shopsmith® lines of abrasives, gave *Fine Woodworking* a tour of its facility near Dayton, Ohio. Production is centered on the "Maker," a 130-yd.-long production line with a couple of two-story ovens. Sandpaper begins as a roll of paper or cloth up to 55 in. wide and 10,000 yd. long that forms its backing. Moving at 30 yd. per minute, the back of the material is printed with a description of the product. Glue is applied to the front via a roller. This first application of glue can be colored to designate the company's code for coarse, medium, or fine abrasive.

Now the electrifying part: The grit comes down a chute to a conveyor belt and passes under a metal bar that gives each particle an electrical charge. The backing passes just over the conveyor belt and the grit jumps onto the sticky surface. And that's not the only cool thing: Not only do the particles space themselves evenly, but also the blunter end of each grain is most attracted to the backing, leaving the pointier end facing out!

The roll of adhesive and grit then heads to a long oven where it is draped on big steel arms to be baked at 120°F to 180°F. The second or "size" coat of glue is applied and baked after the first is cool and hard. This thicker coat comes partway up the abrasive, making it less likely to come away from the backer, without fully coating it and dulling the edges.

After the glue has cured for three days, the roll goes to the flexing machine, which bends and twists the material at sharp angles, creating minuscule fractures in the glue coats to give it greater flexibility and prevent grit loss. Some rolls then receive a stearate coating to reduce surface clogging when the material is used. If hook-and-loop disks are being made from the roll, Velcro backing is applied just after the stearate and then the material is baked one last time. Finally, the cured rolls get die-stamped and sliced into disks, sheets, and belts.

2. ROLL ON GLUE

Color-coded. The face of the backer has the bottom or "make" coat of glue rolled on. It is often color-coded, yellow in this case, to match the grit size of the abrasive.

3. SPRINKLE GRIT

Electrifying process. A hopper with evenly spaced holes in the bottom distributes the abrasive on a conveyor belt (top left). The white abrasive moving from right to left passes under an electrically charged metal rod. This makes each particle stand on end and then jump onto the sticky roll of backing paper when it comes near (bottom left).

4. BEND IT

Microfractures. The stiff roll of sandpaper is bent back and forth at 90° and 45° to make it more flexible and to prevent it from cracking the first time you try to bend it.

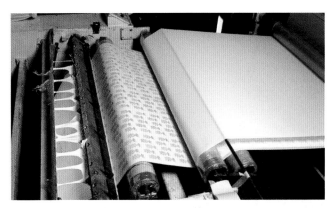

5. BACK IT

Add Velcro for disks. The roll of sandpaper has glue applied to the back and is then mated to the white loop material.

6. CUT IT FOR USE

Disks galore. There's nothing random about the precise stamping of these 5-in. random-orbit disks.

Belts begin as sheets. Wide sheets, with their ends cut on the diagonal, are wrapped around a form and heat is applied to glue the seam.

One loop equals four belts. The abrasive cylinder is spun across fixed knives to create four sanding belts.

Sand between Coats for a Flawless Finish

JEFF JEWITT

Whether you spray, brush, or wipe, one of the keys to a great finish is learning to sand between coats. When I began finishing in the 1970s, there weren't many choices when it came to sanding a finish: Steel wool shed tiny hairs that got embedded in the finish; regular sandpaper (if you could find it above 240-grit) clogged quickly when sanding shellac or lacquer; and if you wanted to flatten defects between coats of finish, you used wet-or-dry paper, which was messy and made it hard to gauge your progress.

Today, not only are there much better choices among consumer-oriented abrasives, but the Internet also has given everyone access to industrial abrasives. I'll narrow down what to use with film-forming finishes like lacquer, varnish, and shellac (in-the-wood 100% oil finishes and thin applications of oil/varnish mixes typically don't require sanding). I'll describe new products to use for dry-sanding between coats, and I'll cover the better use of wet-or-dry paper for sanding the final coat in preparation for the rubbing-out process.

Fine grits and a light touch

Going from sanding bare wood to sanding a finish involves a change of gears. Instead of power-sanding using grits mostly P220 or coarser, you typically hand-sand using grits P320 and finer.

Stearated Sandpaper: No More Clogging

The biggest advance in sanding between coats of finish has been the increasing availability and improving quality of stearated sandpaper. A waxy-feeling powder, zinc or calcium stearate (or a mixture), is incorporated into either aluminum-oxide or silicon-carbide sandpaper. The stearate prevents the dry finish residue from sticking and forming clumps, or corns, or clogging the spaces between the abrasive particles.

Dry-sanding between finish coats is better than wet-sanding because it allows you to see what you're doing much more clearly. If a surface is wet with lubricant, you could be sanding right through the sealer or finish because the lubricant creates an illusion of finish on the wood.

The first coat of finish, whether a purpose-made sealer or just a thinned coat of the final finish, generally leaves a rough surface with raised grain embedded in the finish. At this stage, you aren't flattening the surface, just smoothing it, so there is no need to use a sanding block. Using P320-grit stearated paper, you can make a pad by folding a quarter sheet into thirds. This pad works best if you have to get into corners and other

Myth-buster: New Paper Works with Water-Based Finishes, Too

I've always assumed that stearated sandpaper caused adhesion problems with waterborne finishes. However, after finding little hard evidence, I decided to test several consumer and industrial sandpapers with a variety of waterborne finishes.

I applied one coat of each finish to a separate sample board. When it was dry, I divided the board into sections and sanded this coat smooth with a variety of P320-grit stearated sandpapers. After I removed the sanding residue, I applied another coat of finish and, after 72 hours, evaluated the surface for flow-out and adhesion (below right).

I found no compatibility issues with any of the sandpapers and waterborne finishes. If you use a premium stearated paper, you'll have no problems as long as you remove the residue after sanding.

Tough test reveals the truth. Jewitt applied eight waterborne finishes to a sample board and then sanded sections with different stearated sandpapers before adding a final coat of each finish.

Deep scratches. Jewitt used a special tool to scratch a pattern in the cured finish.

Perfect adhesion. No finish from the scratched area stuck to the tape when he pulled it away.

tight areas. Otherwise, you can just grip a quarter-sheet of paper by wrapping one corner around your pinkie and pinching the other corner between your thumb and index finger. An alternative is pressure-sensitive adhesive (PSA) paper in the same grit (P320) that comes in 2¾-in.-wide rolls. You can tear off only what you need and temporarily stick it to your fingers.

Another option, which costs a bit more, is hook-and-loop pads that allow you to hand-sand using disks designed for random-

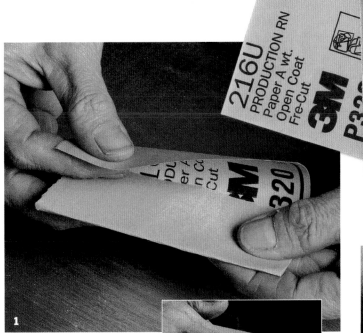

How to handle flat surfaces. Fold a quarter sheet into thirds for tight spots. All the paper can still be used, but there is no grit-on-grit contact.

Sand inside corners. Folding the sheet into thirds allows you to work your way into tight spots.

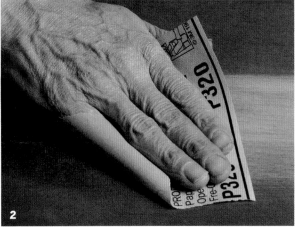

Hand sander. For sanding flat surfaces, just wrap a corner of the sheet around your little finger and grip the opposite corner between your index finger and thumb.

orbit sanders. If the sandpaper starts to load up with debris or corns, I swipe the grit side of the paper against a piece of thick carpet (Berber is best). You also can swipe it on a gray abrasive pad.

It's important to remove the residue after each sanding, or it will cause problems with the next coat of finish. If your finish is oil-based, solvent lacquer, or shellac, dampen a clean cotton or microfiber cloth with naphtha or mineral spirits and wipe away the debris. I prefer naphtha because it evaporates faster and leaves a little less oily residue. For waterborne finishes, I make a mixture of 5% denatured alcohol in tap water (roughly 1 oz. denatured alcohol to 16 oz. water). It's OK to follow the solvent wipe with a tack cloth, but

most tack rags can leave a residue that will interfere with the adhesion of waterborne finishes. One waterborne-friendly tack cloth is 3M™'s item No. 03192.

Higher grits for subsequent coats—

After you have smoothed the sealer coat and applied the first real coat of finish, you should generally use P400- or P600-grit paper to sand; otherwise, you might see tiny sanding scratches in finishes that don't melt into each other, such as oil-based products and most waterborne ones.

You can use a power sander on large, flat surfaces, once you have built up enough finish thickness (at least four to six coats). Use caution when sanding, staying away

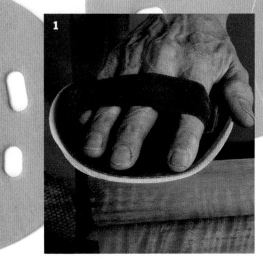

Handy pad. You can hand-sand using disks designed for random-orbit sanders by attaching them to a Velcro-backed pad.

TIP Keep sandpaper clean. Unlike power sanders with onboard dust extraction, hand-sanding can clog the paper quickly. A quick wipe on a carpet remnant gets it clean again.

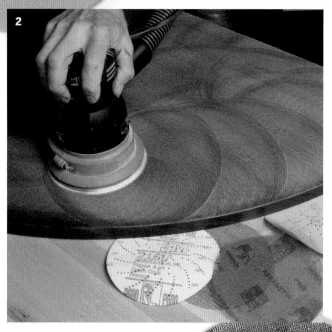

Power-sanding comes later. Once you have applied five or six coats of finish, you can safely use a random-orbit sander equipped with P400-grit disks.

New disks, better dust extraction. Through-the-pad dust extraction has been one of the great innovations in wood finishing. The latest disks work even better and fit all sander models regardless of their hole configuration. Mirka's Abranet is an abrasive-coated mesh (top), while 3M's Clean Sanding disks have spirals of small holes (below).

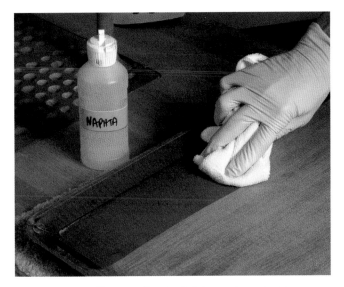

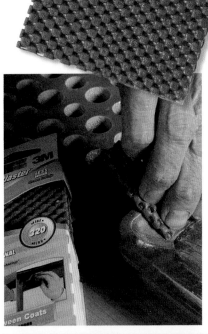

Remove the dust. It is very important to remove all the sanding residue before applying the next coat of finish. For solvent-based finishes, dampen a cloth with naphtha or mineral spirits. The former dries faster (but is harder to spell).

Foam mesh. 3M's SandBlaster™ is a drawer-liner type of foam mesh coated with abrasive. It can be folded over to reach into tight corners or wrapped around curves.

from the edges and using P400-grit paper or higher. For better visibility, I always do this with dust extraction. The better papers out there have holes punched to match the ports on the sanding pad, or are made up of a mesh like Mirka Abranet. An industrial product called Clean Sanding by 3M is disk paper with a spiral progression of small holes for dust extraction.

Special products for moldings, carvings, and turnings—Although you can use sheet sandpaper with shopmade or commercial profiled sanding blocks on gentle profiles, this won't work on sharp curves and other extreme profiles. For these areas, use ultra-flexible sanding sponges or a synthetic steel-wool substitute. Neither of these products has stearates because the face is more open and clogging isn't an issue. After use, most of them can be cleaned with soapy water and reused. I like ultrathin synthetic steel wool, which more easily conforms

Abrasive pads. These pads come in a variety of grits and are thin enough to get into carvings.

Sticky paper. Adhesive-backed sandpaper is useful for sanding narrow surfaces. Simply stick it to a finger.

Sanding sponges. Less flexible than the other products, sanding sponges are good for gentle curves and can be washed out when finished.

to profiles and turnings. Choices include Mirka's Mirlon Total® and 3M's Multi-Flex, both of which are available in a convenient roll, but look for 3M's SandBlaster flexible pads, which last a bit longer and are easier to find at most home centers and hardware stores.

On thin, flat areas like the inside edge of a picture frame or door, hold the pad with your thumb on top and the rest of your fingers underneath. This keeps it level. Or just use a small piece of the PSA paper mentioned earlier.

Wet-or-dry paper still the best for final flattening

Unlike stearated sandpaper, wet-or-dry sandpaper can be either FEPA (P) or CAMI graded. Make sure you know what you're using because a P600 is equivalent to just under a CAMI 400. All FEPA-graded sandpaper should have a P before the grit number; if there is no P, assume it's CAMI grade unless otherwise specified. One feature of wet-or-dry paper is that you can get it in grits up to 2,000 and sometimes higher. If you have any trouble finding it, try an automotive parts supplier.

Wet-or-dry sandpaper is a very sharp and fast-cutting abrasive and works best for removing final defects and flattening the finish prior to rubbing out (where you polish the flattened surface to the desired sheen). You can use mineral spirits, a light mineral oil called paraffin or rubbing oil, or soapy water as a lubricant. Of the three, soapy water is the least messy, though it seems not to cut as fast or as well as the other two. I add a capful of Dawn® dishwashing liquid for every pint (16 oz.) of tap water, and then apply the mixture using a plant mister.

Switch to wet sanding on the final coat. Wet-or-dry sandpaper is the best way to smooth a flat surface prior to rubbing out the finish. Use soapy water as a lubricant and wipe away the slurry to check your progress.

Start with a quarter-sheet of P600-grit paper wrapped around a cork, or a cork-faced, block. Spray some lubricant on the surface and begin sanding with the grain if possible. On a top, I typically rub the outside 3 in. first so I can focus on keeping the block flat and not tipping it off an edge (that happens naturally with my arm motion if I'm taking a long sweep from one end to the other). Once I've gone around a few times, I come back and do the center. Wipe away the slurry and examine the surface. You're done when the surface looks about 80% to 90% dull. Don't try to make the entire surface perfectly dull because you'll probably sand through the finish.

After using the wet-or-dry sandpaper, you can follow up with paste wax applied with 0000 steel wool for a satin finish. An alternative to steel wool is a very fine abrasive foam pad such as Mirka's Abralon. The 1,000-, 2,000-, and 4,000-grits can be used for sheens ranging from dull to satin. You don't need compounds or polishes with these products.

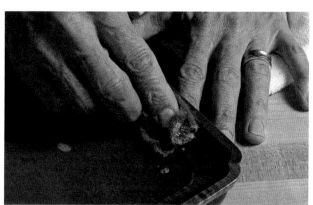

Tight curves. Use 0000 steel wool lubricated with soapy water to remove the gloss on curved surfaces.

Finish up with wax. Apply some paste wax with Liberon's 0000 steel wool and then buff the surface with a cotton cloth for a smooth, satin finish.

Easiest Finish? Danish Oil

GREG ARCENEAUX

Like many woodworkers, part of the reason I make furniture is that I love the natural beauty of wood. That's why I like Danish oil finishes. A mix of varnish and either linseed or tung oil, they provide protection without obscuring the color and grain of the wood. And when you touch the piece it still feels like wood. A few coats of Danish oil, topped off with a coat of wax, give wood a depth, luster, and warmth that can't be beat.

As if that weren't enough to recommend them, Danish oils are also easy to apply. Just wipe or brush them on—you really can't mess that up. And then, after about an hour, wipe off any excess that is still on the wood's surface. Because there really isn't a film drying on the surface, dust nibs aren't a serious problem. Rubbing with steel wool between coats gets rid of them.

I've tried many Danish oil finishes through the years. Early in my career, I brewed my own, but these were either troublesome to make or grew soft and moldy in the humid Louisiana climate. I then tried manufactured Danish oils. I've used a lot of them, but Deft Danish oil was my favorite. Unfortunately, it has been discontinued. But Watco Danish Oil is a good alternative. The techniques in this article work with any Danish oil.

Surface prep is the critical first step. A finish won't look good unless the wood beneath does, too. Arceneaux uses P80-grit sandpaper to remove machine marks and then P120-grit. Next, wet the entire surface with water to raise the grain, and let it dry completely before the last round of sanding (P220-grit).

Power-sand everything you can. On his Louisiana Creole table, Arceneaux used a random-orbit sander on the top, the base (after assembly), and the drawer.

Save hand-sanding for the edges and details. A folded piece of sandpaper preserves crisp lines and gets into the tightest corner.

Start with a silky surface

There is at least one truth in woodworking: No finish can hide a poorly surfaced board. So, before you break out any finish, including Danish oils, grab the sandpaper and expend some elbow grease to create a defect-free and smooth surface. After years of finishing furniture, I've found that three grits are all you need. Start with P80-grit, then move on to P120-grit. Then wet down the surface with water to raise the grain. After it's dry, complete the sanding with P220-grit. There's nothing fussy about this process, and it gets the job done.

Three coats is all it takes

When you're done sanding, you can apply the first coat of Danish oil. Three coats creates a durable and beautiful finish.

I use a brush to get the oil on because brushes hold more finish than rags do. They also get into corners, moldings, and edge profiles better. Flood the surface with oil, then stand back and watch for a bit. Some areas of the wood will be thirstier than

others and will soak up more finish. You can spot them because they have a duller sheen. Reapply oil to these areas until they can't drink in any more.

After about 45 to 60 minutes, thoroughly wipe the surface with a clean rag to remove any oil that remains. Then, for the next 30 minutes, check the surface periodically for dots of oil seeping back out. Wipe off any
(Continued on p. 72)

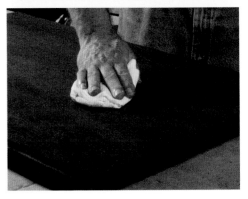

Brush on the oil. Don't be timid. The grain is going to really soak it up, so lay down a heavy coat. Then watch the surface for dull areas, where the oil has been completely absorbed. Add more oil to these areas until they are full (top). Finally, wipe off the excess when the oil begins to get tacky, about 45 to 60 minutes after you first applied it (above).

Application couldn't be easier. It's almost impossible to mess this up. And as long as you wipe off the excess within an hour, you won't.

Steel-wool rubdown. It takes the place of wet-sanding. After a coat has dried overnight, prepare for the next coat by rubbing the surface with steel wool, which helps to build a beautiful luster in the final coat with no worries of going through the finish. Arceneaux uses 000 steel wool after the first two coats, and 0000 after the third.

Wipe away debris. Steel wool leaves a trail of dust. Remove it with a clean rag.

Clean out tight spots with a brush. The bristles of an unused brush knock steel-wool dust from corners, moldings, and routed profiles.

For repeat coats, repeat the steps. Three coats is all you need to create a finish that protects without obscuring the wood. Wipe off the excess after every coat. Always use a clean rag, and do it when the oil is just getting a bit sticky (left). Use the steel wool between every coat (above) and finish with wax (below).

Wax adds depth and patina.
Arceneaux uses LakeOne®
Buffing Wax in dark oak, which
can be brushed on and gives
most woods a "lived-in" look.
For light-color woods, use a
light-color wax.

Brush on, buff off. A brush is
faster than a rag and also does
a better job getting into corners,
edge profiles, and other details. A
clean, soft rag is the right tool for
buffing. Don't start until the wax
has dried enough to haze over.

that you find. If they're tough to get off, dab
some fresh oil onto them. This reactivates the
finish and makes it easy to wipe off. If you
find a dry spot after that first 30 minutes, use
P220-grit sandpaper to remove it. Let it dry
overnight.

The next day, work the entire surface with
000 steel wool. Wipe the surface with a clean
rag to remove the dust, and use a paintbrush
to get the steel-wool dust out of moldings,
corners, and any other tight spots. The
second and third coats go on like the first.
The only change comes after the third coat,
when I use 0000 steel wool.

Top it off with wax

As nice as this finish looks on its own, a
coat of wax gives it a nice depth and feel.
I've experimented with just as many waxes
through the years as I have Danish oils.
My favorite is LakeOne Buffing Wax (www.
alliedpiano.com). It can be brushed on, which
speeds up the process and makes it easy to
get the wax into moldings and carved details.
The dark oak version gives furniture a lovely
patina. After applying the wax, let it dry until
it becomes a bit hazy, and then buff it with a
clean rag.

Get Better Results with Polyurethane

BEN BLACKMAR

I've tried all kinds of finishes in my woodworking career, from beautiful but tedious hand-rubbed oils to quick but expensive sprayed-on lacquers. Nowadays, the finish that I use most often is one of the simplest and most widely available commercial products out there—polyurethane. The finish has significant advantages. First, poly is oil-based, which makes it extremely durable and resistant to water stains. Because of this, it is ideal for tabletops and cabinetry. Poly also cures hard much more quickly than oil, which means you'll be finished in days rather than weeks and with fewer coats.

My approach calls for two different satin-gloss polyurethane products—a fast-drying version of the standard brush-on product and the thin, wiping variety. I start with a thin coat of wipe-on to seal the surface, followed by several brushed-on coats to build a durable protective film. Then, instead of applying wax, I complete the process with another thin coat or two of wipe-on to perfect the satiny, medium sheen. Here's how I do it.

Two products, one finish. Blackmar starts with a sealer coat of thin, wipe-on polyurethane, then builds up a durable film with two coats of brush-on poly. He follows it with more wipe-on poly.

First coat seals the surface

To prepare the surface, I first remove all machine marks by sanding up to P150-grit with a random-orbit sander. I follow this by hand-sanding with a block, using P220-grit, until the surface is uniformly flat and smooth, with no visible scratches.

Last, I use the P220-grit to break the edges. A softened corner is easier to finish, nicer to the touch, and more resistant to denting and wear. Afterward, gently remove the dust with an air compressor or wipe down the piece with a dry, lint-free cotton cloth.

Careful prep is critical. Start by sanding the surfaces smooth. Sand to P150-grit with a random-orbit sander followed by a sanding block to P220-grit, working in the direction of the grain.

Break the edges. Blackmar uses folded P220-grit sandpaper to ease the corners on the top, the legs, and the undersides of the aprons.

Seal inside with shellac. To avoid persistent odors from the polyurethane, Blackmar seals the inside of drawer compartments with shellac.

Wipe on the poly. A thin application of wipe-on poly seals the wood in preparation for the thicker, brushed-on coats. Soak a cloth with wipe-on poly (right) and apply to the entire piece (right). Nitrile gloves keep the finish off your skin.

Brushing adds protection. The heavier brush-on product quickly builds a clear protective film. Apply two coats, then sand to flatten.

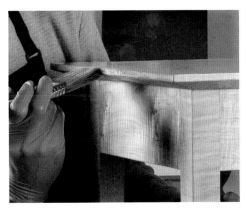

Don't overload the brush. It should hold enough finish to keep a wet edge while applying a relatively light coat. Lightly brush away any drips on the top's edge. Apply two coats.

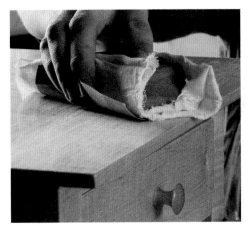

Remove the brush marks. After applying two coats, sand the surface with a block and P220-grit paper to flatten brush marks and other inconsistencies. Blackmar softens the block with a layer of cloth and uses stearated paper designed not to clog.

I begin applying the finish with a thin coat of wipe-on poly to penetrate and seal the surface. Use a lint-free cotton cloth. Saturate the cloth with finish and wipe it on liberally. Then use a clean, dry cloth to remove any excess. Let the finish dry for several hours.

Be sure to dispose of your used rags properly to avoid the possibility of starting a fire. Before tossing them, dry the rags by spreading them out individually on a flat surface or draping them over the rim of a trash barrel.

Rubdown before the topcoat. Rub down the surface with steel wool to level any remaining imperfections.

Thicker coats build a protective film

The next two coats get brushed on so you
can easily build an even, durable layer. In a
warm shop, the "fast-drying" finish lets you
lay down these two coats in one day—if you
start early enough.

To ensure a smooth coat that is relatively
free of brush marks, use a good-quality,
natural-bristle brush. I've gotten great results
with a brush designed for oil paint available
at home centers. Brush on a thin but wet
coat, quickly smoothing out any runs or
drips as you go.

To test whether the first coat is dry enough
to continue, brush the surface with the
back of a finger in an inconspicuous place.
If you leave no marks, it is safe to continue.
Apply the second coat, let it dry, then lightly
hand-sand the surfaces with P220-grit
paper on a block to remove brush marks and
other inconsistencies. Work with the grain.
Afterward, wipe away the dust and lightly
rub down the entire piece with #0000 steel

Wipe on the final coat. Use a rag to apply
the top layer of finish, one thin coat at a
time. Let these coats (two or three) dry
thoroughly before judging the sheen, which
should cure to a uniform satin appearance
with no need for waxing.

TIP Burnish with paper. A folded sheet of white paper is just abrasive enough to remove any dust nibs without scratching the finished surface.

wool. Work with the grain to flatten and create a straight rub pattern on each surface, then wipe away the dust again.

The topcoats go on with a rag

For the topcoats, I use wipe-on poly to create an even, thin layer. These coats dry quickly, so work systematically, smoothing out the most recently applied finish before moving on. Avoid wiping areas you've already covered, even if they appear dry.

Four to six hours after the first coat, when it is dry to the touch, apply another coat the same way. After two or three thin coats, any scratches or marks left from the steel wool should be gone.

Wait a day or two before making a final judgment on the sheen's uniformity. As the last layer cures and hardens, the apparent sheen across the piece will equalize. If you're not satisfied, repeat the steel-wool step and wipe on more poly.

Tabletop Finish with a Hand-Rubbed Feel

MARK SCHOFIELD

Start with a coat of shellac. A thin washcoat of shellac reduces blotching. Use premixed shellac or dissolve some flakes in denatured alcohol, but avoid waxy shellac, which will prevent the subsequent coat of polyurethane from adhering.

Years ago when I wrote the article "One Editor's Foolproof Finish" that appeared in *Fine Woodworking* #196, several readers asked whether the wipe-on finish I described would be suitable for kitchen cabinets or dining tables. I replied that while you could build up the extra protection these surfaces need by wiping on many more coats of the gel polyurethane, it would be far quicker to brush on several coats of liquid polyurethane and then switch to the wipe-on gel for the final few coats. In

Wipe on a thin coat. Make a couple of passes to seal the wood with shellac. Whether you use a French-polishing-style pad or folded-up cotton cloth, adding the shellac with a squeeze bottle is quick and controllable.

this way, you get the rapid build of a brushed finish, without any brush marks or dust nibs in the final surface.

This approach to a durable yet smooth finish is so foolproof, we decided to share it with all of our readers in this step-by-step article. By the way, because it starts with a quick washcoat of shellac, it is also a great finish for pieces made from blotch-prone woods, such as this cherry dining table by Gary Rogowski. The table also demonstrates how this finish can be used in tandem with my original wipe-on-only Foolproof Finish: I used the durable finish on the tabletop, where food and liquids will be a hazard, and on the feet, which are likely to be rubbed by shoes. But I used the simpler finish on the rest of the piece.

Sand carefully, then seal

Although this won't be a high-gloss finish that magnifies every ripple or void in the surface, we're still dealing with an eye-catching large, flat surface, so good preparation is essential.

Either flatten and smooth the tabletop using handplanes and a scraper or if you are more comfortable with a random-orbit sander, start at P100-grit and work your way up to P220-grit, then hand-sand with the grain using the final grit. Remove the dust using a vacuum or compressed air to clean out the pores.

The next step is to apply a thin coat of shellac to the whole piece. As well as greatly reducing the likelihood of blotching, the shellac gives the wood a slightly warmer

A light touch. Lay on a coat of polyurethane starting a few inches from one edge and brushing off the opposite edge. Use a light touch, holding the brush at about 45° to the surface. After the first pass, land the brush just inside the far end and return, smoothing the strip of wet finish until you cover the small dry area and go lightly off the end. By brushing off the ends and not onto them, you avoid having finish run down the edges.

Brushed poly builds a base. Three or four coats of liquid polyurethane, sanded smooth between coats, are enough to give the wood real protection without a thick, plastic look.

tone and lets you build a sheen faster with the gel finish. You may have heard that polyurethane will not adhere to shellac. This is true if you use shellac containing wax, such as Zinsser's clear or amber Bulls Eye Shellac. Polyurethane will adhere perfectly to dewaxed shellac such as Zinsser's SealCoat or your own mixture using dewaxed shellac flakes.

Mix a 1-lb. to 1½-lb. cut (dilute the SealCoat by about a third with denatured alcohol). You can apply the shellac with a natural or synthetic filament brush, but I find it just as quick (and easier on vertical surfaces) to wipe on the shellac with a cotton cloth. It also requires less sanding afterward.

Let the shellac dry for two to four hours depending on the temperature and the humidity, and then lightly sand the surface

with P320-grit paper wrapped around a cork or cork-faced block. All you are doing is removing any particles, dust nibs, etc., to leave a smooth surface. Wipe and vacuum away the dust.

Brush polyurethane to add toughness

Because you won't be brushing on the final coats, you don't need a really expensive brush that leaves a perfect surface. A $10 to $20 natural-bristle brush, 2 in. or 2½ in. wide, works fine for most surfaces. If you have no experience brushing finishes, or if your attempts have been below par, this is a painless way to build your brushing skills and confidence.

You can use any brand of oil-based gloss polyurethane, even those recommended for floors, but the viscosity between different

How to sand efficiently. Fine P320-grit sandpaper has a short life span, so move to a fresh piece as soon as it stops cutting. A quick way to unclog the sandpaper is to wipe it on a remnant of carpet. Stiff and coarse weaves work best. Don't try to sand out every small depression in the surface.

Layers of protection. The subsequent coats of polyurethane are applied in the same way. Moving the brush slowly (above left) minimizes bubbles in the finish. You are not looking for a perfectly flat surface, but high points and depressions should be well covered with finish (above right).

brands varies greatly. The Minwax Fast-Drying Polyurethane I used is about the consistency of 1% or 2% milk and can be used straight from the can. If your finish is closer to heavy cream, then thin it with mineral spirits.

You need to apply a roughly equal thickness of finish to both sides of the top to prevent uneven moisture changes, which cause cupping and warping. Start with the underside of the table, a good place to practice your brushing technique where the appearance is less important. Brush on three coats. You don't need to sand between coats as long as you apply the next coat within 24 hours.

Final sanding. Use P400-grit sandpaper to smooth the final coat of brushed-on poly. Don't try to sand down to a perfectly flat surface.

As soon as the underside is finished, start on the top. Let the first coat cure overnight, then sand the surface with P320-grit paper. Use stearated paper, which is designed to resist becoming clogged with finish. Most sandpaper is stearated (it has a slightly white, opaque look), but avoid garnet paper designed for bare wood. Even stearated paper clogs fairly quickly, so follow finishing expert Jeff Jewitt's advice and wipe the paper frequently on a carpet remnant.

Don't overuse the sandpaper. It is meant to be disposable, and you'll get much better results if you switch to a new piece as soon as the paper no longer feels rough or becomes clogged almost instantly.

When the whole surface feels smooth to the touch, including the edges, remove the dust with a vacuum. You should apply a minimum of three coats. Sand intermediate coats with P320-grit paper, but sand the last one with P400-grit.

Unlike a high-gloss, rubbed-out finish, you don't need to make the surface dead-flat before applying the satin gel poly, so don't try to sand away all the small, shiny depressions. However, the shininess will

Rub with steel wool. To dull the small, shiny depressions and leave the surface with an even sheen, rub the surface with good-quality 0000 steel wool.

show through, so after sanding rub the surface with the grain using Liberon 0000 steel wool to dull these spots and to give the whole surface an even scratch pattern. Use raking light to check your progress. It is worth ordering the Liberon steel wool (www.highlandwoodworking.com) because it lasts longer, produces better results, and sheds less than the product found in hardware stores.

Gel poly removes topcoat terror

After you carefully vacuum away all the remnants of steel wool, the surface should look pretty good—smooth, with a fairly even sheen. Normally, you would brush on the final coat of polyurethane and leave it, risking dust nibs and brush marks. With my approach, you'll top off the surface by wiping on and buffing off several coats of gel finish (see the photos on p. 84). These super-thin coats dry so quickly that dust doesn't have time to settle on them. Again, the brand doesn't matter: I've had good results with Petri's Gel Poly Finish and the one I'm using here, General Finishes' Gel Topcoat. They are both satin polyurethane turned into a gel.

Take a piece of cotton cloth about 4 in. square and dab some gel varnish onto it with a small stick. Wipe the gel onto the surface in a circular motion. Don't try to cover more than 2 to 3 sq. ft. before immediately coming back with a larger piece of clean cotton cloth and buffing the surface in quick strokes with the grain. If you wait too long and the surface becomes sticky, wipe on a little more gel to reactivate the finish and then immediately buff the surface. What you are doing is obscuring the fine scratches left by the steel wool. However, you are applying an extremely thin coat of finish, so be prepared to apply at least three coats. The directions on the can will probably say to wait overnight between coats, but in warm, dry conditions, eight hours is plenty.

For the areas of the table that don't need the extra protection of the brushed-on polyurethane, just wipe on the gel finish as described above. Four or five coats should be sufficient to get a sheen that matches the brushed areas.

Adding a coat of wax is optional. On pieces likely to be handled regularly, I use it as much for the feel as any extra protection. But on a dining table likely to be wiped frequently with a damp cloth, wax is a waste of time.

Tips for gel poly. Use a stirring stick to place some of the thick finish on a small piece of cotton cloth (top left). Dipping the cloth is too messy. Apply the gel in a circular motion until you've covered a few square feet in an even layer (left). Buff off the surplus finish right away using quick, firm strokes and turning frequently to a fresh section of cotton cloth. Repeat until the whole tabletop is done. Look at how happy you'll be with your flawless finish (below).

Wiping Varnishes, Head to Head

MARK SCHOFIELD

The best can do it all. Some varnishes can be wiped on for easy application (left) or brushed on a tabletop for added protection (top right). As a bonus, if that brushed surface is uneven or has a lot of dust in it, you can sand lightly and then add a last wiped-on coat (above right) for a flawless final surface.

It's no surprise that so many wood-workers love wiped-on finishes: They are hard to mess up, and the oil soaks in and highlights the carefully chosen hardwood below, adding an elegantly low sheen. But a thin, wiped-on finish doesn't offer enough protection for a high-wear area such as a tabletop or chair seat. In those cases, you reach for a brush to build a thicker finish.

That's why the ideal finish could be brushed and wiped on equally well. You could use that one finish in a variety of combinations, such as wiping it on a table base where there's less wear, and brushing it on the top for durability. And with only a single can on the shelf, you would save money and waste less.

There are finishes that promise to work for brushing and wiping. Officially classed as "wiping varnishes," they basically are oil-based varnishes that are thinned with solvent, and then, unfortunately, sold under a bewildering variety of names.

The wrinkle test. The common test for a finish's ability to cure as a film is to drop some into a shallow dish and wait.

Is It a Wiping Varnish?

Most finishes, if thin enough, can be wiped on. But for a finish to be brushed successfully, it must cure level and hard when applied as a thicker film. A simple "wrinkle" test tells the tale.

True wiping varnish. All but one of the finishes cured hard and level, proving they would work when brushed.

Oil finish. An oil finish or oil-varnish blend, when dry, will have a wrinkled or rubbery surface, which makes it unsuitable for brushing.

Fine Woodworking asked me to test these finishes to find out which ones work best for both brushing and wiping. Preparing for this test, I knew it wasn't going to be easy to identify all of the possible candidates. I contacted each relevant finish manufacturer and simply asked which of their products could be both wiped and brushed. Like the names and instructions on the cans, the manufacturers' answers were not very clear. A few were confident their finishes could be applied both ways; a few stated categorically that their wiping finish couldn't be brushed; and some fence-sitters said they didn't recommend brushing "but it would probably work." Based on their answers, I identified 16 finishes to test. Where there were different luster levels available, such as gloss, satin, etc., I went with the gloss version. The only exception was Zar® Ultra Max poly, which was available only as semi-gloss but looked like gloss anyway in practice.

Once I had the finishes in hand, I first made sure that every one was a true wiping varnish, which is simply a thinned varnish, and not an oil-varnish blend or simply oil. After this initial test, one finish—Sam Maloof Poly/Oil Finish—fell out of the running.

How the testing was done

Although I wanted the same thing from each finish—easy application and great results on a

As a wipe-on finish. Schofield wiped and brushed each product on two types of woods: plain cherry and figured maple. Then he evaluated the appearance and toughness of each finish. To start, he divided each cherry sample board down the middle, wiping finish onto one half (the other half was for brushing), letting it soak in, and then wiping it off.

As a brushed varnish. Schofield let each brushed-on coat cure for 24 hours before sanding with P320-grit paper and applying another one. He stopped when the surface was a smooth film with no irregularities.

Sanding between coats. He sanded the first coat of each wiped-on finish with P400-grit paper. All of the finishes sanded easily enough.

As many coats as necessary. He applied as many coats as it took to get an even sheen.

variety of woods—I knew that each product has differences, such as the amount of solids in the finish and therefore how long it takes to build a film. So I treated each one as an individual, working to get the best from it. For the wiped-on samples, I was looking simply for an even sheen. For the brushed-on samples, I wanted to build enough of a film to protect the top of a dining table and create a dead-smooth surface. While inconsistencies in the wood, like pores and minor irregularities from planing or sanding, will show in the surface of a wiped-on finish, I wanted those all to be filled and smoothed out by the brushed-on film. The number of coats it took to achieve each of these results varied (see chart, pp. 90–91), which means that some of these finishes will take longer to apply than others, a factor I weighed as heavily as looks and durability.

I tried each product on two common furniture woods. I used curly maple to see how each finish popped the figure and how its color impacted a pale wood. I also tested each finish on cherry because of its neutral color and popularity. I sanded each board to P220-grit using a random-orbit sander, continuing up to P400-grit for the wipe-on

Color varies. Schofield used the maple samples to evaluate color. The darkest finish was Waterlox (left), while Formby's® Tung Oil Finish (right) added the least color.

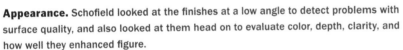

Appearance. Schofield looked at the finishes at a low angle to detect problems with surface quality, and also looked at them head on to evaluate color, depth, clarity, and how well they enhanced figure.

Trouble with oil/water hybrids. The Zar Ultra Max finish (shown) was plagued by fish-eyes when brushed. The Wood Turners Finish left cherry looking gray.

Thick and thin. The best finishes were beautiful both brushed on thick and wiped on thin.

boards. Thinner finishes require a smoother surface for best results.

Wipe-on application varied—Some wiping varnishes get sticky quicker than others. So I wiped on the first coat liberally, allowed it to soak in for the length of time recommended by the manufacturer, and then wiped off the surplus. If no time was specified on the can, I checked each finish after 10 and 15 minutes, wiping it off if it was starting to get sticky, and leaving it for 20 minutes if not.

A coat of oil-based finish needs at least 12 hours to dry before sanding. To be safe, I waited 24 hours before sanding the first coat with P400-grit paper and a cork-faced block. Then I vacuumed off the dust and wiped on more coats, waiting 24 hours each time.

Additional tests for brushed finishes

I chose a natural China-bristle brush for the brushing test, except for the two oil/water hybrids, where I used a foam brush. I allowed the first coat to dry 24 hours before sanding. A brushed surface is a little bumpier than a wiped one, so I sanded with P320-grit. I repeated these steps, sanding each coat, until I was happy with the look.

After letting the finishes cure for a week, I evaluated them for clarity, depth, and how well they enhanced the wood's figure and natural shimmer. I then rubbed them out with steel wool and wax to better represent a typical final surface, and tested them for durability and protection. All of the finishes rubbed out fairly easily.

To determine wear-resistance, I used a set of 12 pencils with leads graduated from a soft 6b to a hard 4h to try to scratch the surface. All the finishes were at least moderately scratch-resistant, but a few offered a higher level of hardness. To see if the brushed-on finishes offered enough protection for a tabletop, I left some red wine under a glass for 24 hours on each maple board. The good news is that all 15 finishes were undamaged.

There was also some variation in the amount of color that the finishes imparted on the maple, whether brushed or wiped. The darkest finish was the Waterlox, followed closely by the Sutherland Welles® Wiping Varnish and the Zar Tung Oil Wipe-On Finish. The finish that turned the maple least yellow was Formby's Tung Oil Finish, followed closely by Minwax Wipe-On Poly.

Protection. To test the impermeability of the brushed finishes, Schofield dipped the base of a glass in red wine and left it on a sample board for 24 hours. In every case, the dried wine simply wiped off (below), leaving no trace.

Durability. Using a set of pencils with 12 levels of hardness, Schofield attempted to scratch each finish.

Toughness varied. Most of the finishes were scratched by the hardest pencils, but a few were unblemished.

Wiping Varnishes: The Ratings

To come out on top, a finish had to wipe and brush well, beautify the wood, and produce the desired level of sheen and protection in the fewest possible coats.

Product	Coats needed		Surface quality		Shimmer/ depth*	Figure**	Scratch test
	Wiping	Brushing	Wiping	Brushing			
Formby's Tung Oil Finish	3 to 4	4	Excellent	Very good	Excellent	Excellent	Good
BEST OVERALL General Finishes Arm-R-Seal	3	3	Excellent	Excellent	Excellent	Excellent	Very good
General Finishes Seal-A-Cell	3 to 4	4	Very good	Very good	Excellent	Very good	Good
General Finishes Wood Turners Finish	3	4	Fair	Very good	Fair	Very good	Good
Minwax Antique Oil Finish	3 to 4	5	Good	Good	Very good	Excellent	Good
BEST VALUE Minwax Fast-Drying Polyurethane	3 to 4	3	Excellent	Excellent	Excellent	Excellent	Very good
Minwax Tung Oil Finish	3 to 4	4	Excellent	Very good	Excellent	Excellent	Good
Minwax Wipe-On Poly	3 to 4	5	Very good	Very good	Excellent	Excellent	Good
Phoenix Finish-All™	4	5	Fair	Very good	Fair	Very good	Good
Sutherland Welles Murdoch's Hard Sealer™	5	4	Fair	Good	Fair	Good	Good
Sutherland Welles Wiping Varnish	2	3	Good	Excellent	Excellent	Excellent	Excellent
Watco Wipe-On Poly	3	4	Very good	Very good	Excellent	Excellent	Good
Waterlox Original Sealer/Finish	4	5	Good	Very good	Excellent	Excellent	Good
Zar Tung Oil Wipe-On Finish	3	3	Excellent	Very good	Excellent	Excellent	Excellent
Zar Ultra Max Wipe-On Poly	4	5	Poor	Poor	Fair	Very good	Excellent

* Tested on cherry   ** Tested on curly maple

General
Finishes
Arm-R-Seal

BEST OVERALL
AUTHOR'S CHOICE

Minwax
Fast-Drying
Polyurethane

BEST VALUE
AUTHOR'S CHOICE

Comments

Takes one more coat than the winners, but results are beautiful. Adds the least color to light woods.

Gives beautiful results with only three coats, wiped or brushed. More scratch-resistant than most.

Very thin finish builds slowly but has good depth and shimmer. Not able to build as thick a film as others.

Oil/water hybrid. Finish dries fast and sands easily but doesn't penetrate or add shimmer. Also, gray-looking on maple.

Thin finish builds very slowly, especially when brushed. Pops figure well.

Designed for brushing but also wipes easily. Builds quickly with beautiful results and above-average toughness.

Top-notch results but builds slower than some and offers moderate scratch-resistance.

Thin finish requires more coats to build when brushing but yields good results. Second-least color change on maple.

More of a sealer than a finish. Required many coats and results were dull.

More of a sealer than a finish. Never really built whether wiped or brushed on.

Thick, fast-building, beautiful, and tough. Best brushed finish in test but hard to wipe on evenly.

Good build and great looks but more dust nibs than others, perhaps due to longer drying time.

Darkest finish was slow to build. Even five brushed coats left a somewhat irregular finish.

Good build but very thick. Brushed-on coats were a little uneven. Tied for highest scratch-resistance.

Hybrid oil-water mix. Too sticky for wiping evenly, and brushed-on coats became a mass of fish-eyes (dimples).

The bottom line

While this test revealed a few specialists— thin finishes that wipe beautifully but don't build much, and thick finishes that brush on clear and tough—I was looking for finishes that do it all. A number of these products fill the bill, but two edged out the rest when all factors were considered. General Finishes Arm-R-Seal is my pick for the Best Overall finish. It applies quickly and easily by brush or rag, builds quickly with fewer coats than most, looks great thick or thin, and rubs out easily with steel wool.

On sale for as low as $10 a quart, Minwax Fast-Drying Polyurethane is a steal. Meant for brushing, its low viscosity also makes it excellent for wiping. You might have to wipe on an extra coat compared to the Arm-R-Seal, but the results are almost identical, the price is lower, and the finish is more widely available.

Wiping Varnish: The Only Finish You'll Ever Need

MICHAEL PEKOVICH

For me, the ideal finish for handmade furniture is a silky smooth, low-luster finish that lets the beauty of the wood shine through. Over the years, I've tried countless products and techniques trying to achieve this look. Some required elbow grease and homemade concoctions. Some took weeks to apply. Some looked great at first only to fade over time.

Finally, I've found a finish that gives me the durability and flawless look I want along with easy application. The answer is wiping varnish. It's a versatile finish that is thin enough to wipe on but dries hard even when applied in thicker coats. This allows me to build the finish quickly, then end with thin coats that give me just the look I want. My brand of choice is Waterlox, a tung-oil-based varnish. It builds quickly, levels well when brushed on, and adds a beautiful amber tone to the work.

In finishing, the technique is just as important as the product, and the directions on the back of the can just don't cut it. I'll share the simple steps I've discovered for fast, dependable results. I'll also show you how to apply wiping varnish for a high-luster look, suitable for high-style furniture.

Simple steps to a flawless finish

As opposed to oil finishes, which must go on in thin coats, wiping varnish lets you build the finish fast, level it, then continue with

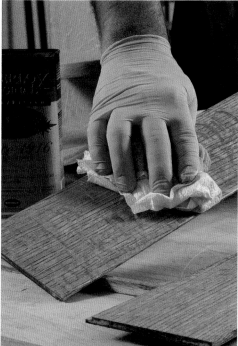

A brush is fast. It allows you to apply a heavy coat evenly, and the bristles let you work into the corners. Any brush will do. Wipe away the excess finish, working in the direction of the grain.

thin coats that dry quickly. One secret to a durable finish is to build to a little higher gloss than you're aiming for, then rub it out to a lower luster. This way you have a thick enough film for adequate protection with the sheen you want.

Step 1: Flood it on and wipe it off

For this thin-film approach to work, careful surface prep is crucial to remove any mill marks, sanding scratches, or tearout. Be sure to sand to P320-grit, or higher for blotch-prone woods.

With that done, begin applying the finish by brushing on a liberal coat. The finish will penetrate the bare wood, so apply more finish to any areas that begin to look dry. After 10 minutes or so, wipe the entire surface dry.

On open-pored woods like oak, the soaked-in finish can sometimes seep back out of the pores for a few minutes. Wipe away these shiny damp spots; they're tough to remove later. Let this coat dry overnight.

Apply the finish with circular strokes. This helps to ensure an even coat (top). Smooth the finish with straight strokes (above). Follow the grain along the length of the workpiece for the smoothest application.

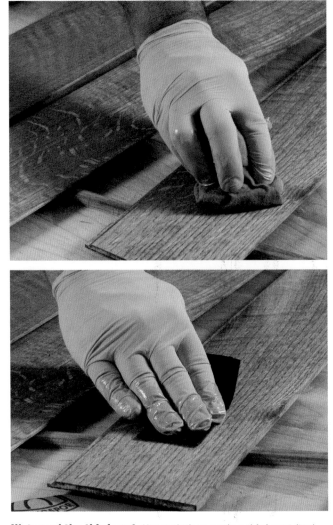

Wet-sand the third coat. Use a cloth to apply a third coat (top), then use folded sandpaper to work the wet finish with the grain (above). Afterward, use the cloth again to even out the still-damp finish, as you did in Step 2.

Step 2: Wipe on a coat and leave it

The second coat also will go on heavy, but this time you'll leave more of it behind. So now you should switch to a clean cotton cloth, as wiping is easier to control than brushing.

After coating the surface with circular strokes, wipe the finish gently in the direction of the grain, working to level it without wiping it off. Let it dry overnight.

Step 3: Level the surface

Once the first two coats have dried, there may be areas of raised grain or dust nibs, so it's important to smooth the surface. The easiest way is to apply a thin third coat of finish and wet-sand it with P400-grit paper. The result is a sealed, smooth starting point from which to begin applying the remaining coats. Wet-sanding lubricates the sandpaper and prevents clogging, allowing the paper to cut more aggressively while still leaving a fine scratch pattern. Let it dry overnight.

Work in a thin coat. Apply the finish in a circular motion, working it into the wood in a thin layer (above). Then wipe lightly with the grain (right). The thin coats should dry quickly enough to allow a couple of coats a day.

Step 4: Add a few thin coats

With the foundation coats applied and the surface smoothed, continue building the finish in a series of thin coats that level easily and dry quickly enough to avoid dust nibs.

Again, start with a circular motion to apply the varnish. Then follow the grain with light strokes to even out the finish without completely wiping it off, and allow it to dry. Four to six of these light coats should build up enough finish to protect the wood without encasing it in a heavy film.

My Favorite Wiping Varnish

When I proposed featuring Waterlox in this article, my editor asked how it stacks up to similar finishes.

To find out, I compared Waterlox Original and three other wipe-on finishes: Zar Tung Oil Wipe-on Finish, Sutherland Welles Ltd. Wiping Varnish, and Minwax Wipe-on Poly. I applied each finish to a cherry sample board using the two methods in this article. I noted how fast each one built, how well it leveled, and how each finish toned the wood.

In the wipe-on test, each finish performed well. The Waterlox, Zar, and Sutherland Welles finishes built faster and created a darker tone than the Minwax. The Waterlox was darkest. The brush-on test showed similar results, but Waterlox leveled the best.

Any of these products will yield good results, but I'll stay with Waterlox. It builds quickly, levels well, and its darker tone complements the oak, cherry, and mahogany I typically work with. For lighter wood like maple that I wanted to keep light, I'd try Minwax Wipe-on Poly.

Step 5: Rub it out with steel wool

For years, I applied wax with steel wool. Why not? It killed two birds with one stone, rubbing out and waxing the piece in one step. Trouble is, wax makes it hard to see the scratch pattern created by the steel wool, and it's easy to end up with an uneven sheen.

Rubbing out the surface first with steel wool alone lets you see what you're doing. Afterward, you can apply the wax with a cloth. For broad, flat surfaces, you can also wrap the 0000 steel wool around a cork-faced sanding block. Wipe the surface clean to check your progress. The finished result should be a dull, even sheen.

Step 6: Wax is the final touch

A coat of wax will protect against scuffing and bring out the shine. The solvents in wax can soften a fresh finish, so let the finish cure for a week or so before applying the wax. When wiping on wax, I dampen the cloth with mineral spirits first. It thins the wax and allows me to apply an even coat that's easier to buff when dry.

Create a wider pad. Start by unrolling the narrow pad and folding it into a square. Work every surface, being careful not to rub through the finish along the edges.

Cleanup is key. Pekovich uses compressed air to clear the corners of steel-wool fragments and dust.

That's the spirit. Dampen the cloth with mineral spirits before charging the cloth with wax.

Work the wax into the wood. The mineral spirits will help the wax spread evenly and thinly (above). Then buff with a soft cloth (right). The surface should have a pleasing satin luster.

Want more protection, or a higher shine?

A higher luster requires a thicker layer of finish. Tabletops do, too. By the way, on open-pored woods like mahogany, you may also need to fill the grain first.

Seal and level the surface as in steps 1 to 3 of the low-luster finish. Then continue building the finish by brushing on heavier coats and letting them dry without wiping. Use an inexpensive foam brush for an even coat on flat surfaces and a rag for everything else. These slower-drying coats gather more dust nibs and need another round of leveling with fine sandpaper followed by steel wool to achieve an even scratch pattern.

For a satin finish, you could follow the steel wool with paste wax and buff. But for a higher polish, use a fine automotive polishing compound applied with a clean cotton cloth. It isn't strictly necessary to apply wax afterward; the luster is already nice. Still, it makes sense to apply wax to tabletops to add scuff resistance.

Build it thicker. A foam brush works fine. Apply the finish in slightly overlapping passes. Don't worry about small bubbles or brush strokes; the finish levels well as it dries.

Sand between coats. Use P600-grit paper wrapped around a cork-faced sanding block to remove any dust nibs and level the finish.

Wet-sand to level the finish. The wood is sealed, so the water won't raise the grain. Use 600-grit paper. For curved parts, skip this step and go right to the steel wool.

Steel wool. Follow the sandpaper with 0000 steel wool. Dip it in water mixed with a few drops of liquid soap for an even scratch pattern. You can stop here for more protection with the same satin finish.

Polish for a higher gloss. The fine abrasives in commercial auto polishes offer a higher luster than steel wool. Squirt some polishing compound onto the surface and buff with a clean rag. Remove the residue with a clean cloth and apply wax.

Make Shellac Your Go-To Finish

MARIO RODRIGUEZ

My first experience with shellac, at age 14, was a disaster. I almost ruined a bookcase I'd built, and I swore off shellac altogether. But in time I learned how to use it correctly, and today shellac is one of my favorite finishes.

It's a cinch to apply, and because it dries so fast, you can apply multiple coats in a day and repair mistakes with ease.

It doesn't take an expert to get great results with shellac. Follow a few simple steps, and you can create a lustrous, satiny finish that makes grain and figure pop, no matter the species.

Fresh, dewaxed shellac is plenty durable

Shellac gets a bad rap for durability, in part because of confusion between waxy and dewaxed versions. Stick with dewaxed shellac; it dries to a hard, impermeable film that protects against heat and moisture and is compatible with all finishes. True, shellac won't hold up against spilled alcohol. But since dewaxed shellac bonds beautifully with every other finish, you can always follow it up with a wipe-on varnish to protect vulnerable surfaces.

Shellac's freshness affects its performance and durability. That's where I went wrong with my bookshelf: I used old shellac and it never fully dried. To be sure it's fresh, buy and mix shellac only as needed. Store it in a cool, dry place, like a basement or refrigerator. If its freshness is in doubt, brush some onto a scrap. If it's still tacky in two hours, it's not fresh.

Choosing the Right Version

Shellac is widely used as a sealer coat under other finishes, but it can produce a striking, low-luster finish on its own. For maximum durability, use dewaxed shellac, whether premixed or flakes. Shellac is most durable when it's fresh, so try to buy only what you'll use in the next few months.

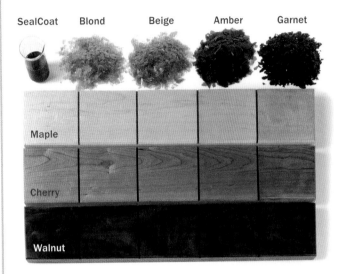

SealCoat   Blond   Beige   Amber   Garnet

Maple

Cherry

Walnut

FLAKES OFFER SAFE, SUBTLE TONES

Dewaxed flakes range in color from clear to amber (orange) to deep reddish browns, like garnet. Unlike dyes and stains, shellac flakes offer a foolproof way to impart warm, subtle tones without any blotching. Color differences are more apparent on lighter woods like maple and cherry than they are on darker woods like walnut (above). Dewaxed flakes are available from online retailers.

PREMIXED IS CONVENIENT

If you want a clear finish that adds just a hint of warmth, Zinsser's SealCoat is the right choice. It's the only dewaxed shellac that's available premixed at home centers and hardware stores. Keep in mind when buying any shellac that if the packaging doesn't specify "dewaxed" or "wax-free," it probably isn't.

Skip the wax. Wax is an ingredient in some shellacs, including Zinsser's "clear"(above) and "amber" products. When waxy shellac dries, the wax allows moisture to permeate the finish, making it less durable.

Use dewaxed instead. Without the wax, shellac dries to a hard film that's impervious to moisture. For premixed, you have one choice: Zinsser's SealCoat.

Thin shellac to suit the project

Whether you're using flakes or premixed shellac, adjust the thickness to suit the job. The "cut" refers to the ratio of flakes to alcohol: Add 1 oz. of flakes to a cup (8 oz.) of alcohol to make a 1-lb. cut, 2 oz. of flakes to a cup for a 2-lb. cut, and so on. If you don't have a scale, you can measure flakes by volume with standard kitchen measuring cups. One ounce by weight is roughly equal to 1 oz. by volume, or ⅛ cup.

For a small project like this end table, mix about a pint of shellac, half at a 1-lb. cut and half at a 1½-lb. cut. Start with a 1-lb. cut as a sealer, to raise the grain and ensure that successive coats build uniformly. Follow with two coats at a 1½-lb. cut to build the finish. I use a 1-lb. cut for the final coat because, with more alcohol, it flows and levels better, which minimizes brush marks.

Zinsser's SealCoat comes in a 2-lb. cut; for a 1-lb. cut, combine one part SealCoat to one part alcohol. For a 1½-lb. cut, mix two parts SealCoat with one part alcohol.

How to Mix Your Own

Grind for speed. Ground flakes dissolve completely in a few hours. If you don't grind them, it's best to give them a full day.

Mix with denatured alcohol. Give the mixture an occasional shake to keep the shellac from congealing at the bottom of the jar.

Strain before brushing. When the flakes are fully dissolved, pour the solution through a medium-mesh paint strainer to remove any impurities.

Denatured alcohol	1-lb. cut	1½-lb. cut	2-lb. cut
1 cup (8 fluid oz.)	1 oz. flakes (by volume)	1½ oz. flakes (by volume)	2 oz. flakes (by volume)

Prep surfaces with sandpaper. Beautiful finishes start with careful prep. All surfaces should be sanded thoroughly to remove machine and mill marks. To ensure uniformity, sand all surfaces, starting at P120-grit and finishing with P220.

Flush between grits. Before moving to a finer grit, flush surfaces with alcohol and wipe them down with a rag to remove any loose abrasive particles, which can leave scratches.

Tack strips elevate the workpiece. Rodriguez uses scraps of plywood with protruding drywall screws to hold the workpiece, allowing him to flip it as needed without marring the finish.

Coat the brush in alcohol first. Whether you're softening an old brush or using a new one, work alcohol into the bristles to help the brush flow smoothly and keep shellac from drying in the reservoir (the hollow area where the bristles meet the metal ferrule).

Hit the edges first. When brushing narrow edges with a big brush, drips are likely to form on adjacent surfaces. If you brush the edges first, drips will form on the large, flat, dry surfaces, where they can be cleaned up quickly and easily.

Wipe-On Alternative

Where brushing would cause excessive drips, like on a chair splat (right), shellac can be applied with a pad.

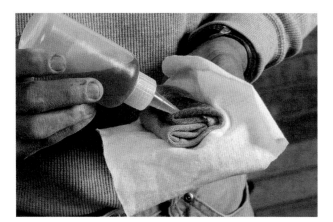

Charge the pad. Fold up a piece of wool (or other absorbent cloth) and place it at the center of a lint-free cotton rag. Use a squeeze bottle to fill the wool until it's soaked but not dripping.

Slow but safe. Wrap the pad so its surface is wrinkle-free. The wool releases a thin coat of shellac through the cotton onto the surface, so it takes more coats to achieve the same look as parts that have been brushed. Seal the pad in a glass jar to keep it supple between coats.

Brush on a sealer coat. Brush on a coat of 1-lb. cut shellac to raise the grain and seal the surface, creating a level foundation for subsequent coats. In two hours, it can be sanded with P320-grit paper.

Don't look back. Apply shellac in long, continuous strokes with little overlap. If you miss a spot, don't go back. "Backbrushing" into drying finish will leave deep brush marks. Subsequent coats will cover small missed spots without any problem.

Prep surfaces and seal

Sand all surfaces, working from P120-grit to P150, then P220. Between grits, flush the surface with alcohol to remove lingering abrasive particles and reveal any surface flaws that might need fixing.

I apply shellac with a brush because it builds the finish in fewer coats than a rag. I use a 2-in. Chinex brush, but natural China bristle or Taklon work well, too. To help avoid drips and detect brush marks and other imperfections, lay parts flat if possible.

To start, apply one coat of 1-lb. cut shellac as a sealer. Hit the edges first. Then, for flat surfaces, load the brush and tap the tips of the bristles on the inside of the container so that it's full but not dripping. To avoid reaching over drying finish, start at a far corner and

TIP Brush care is easy. To store your brush, give it a few dips in alcohol and wrap it in a paper sleeve to keep the bristles straight and clean. The shellac that remains in the bristles will harden, further protecting the brush's shape during storage. When you're ready to use it again, just soak it in alcohol to soften it up.

Sand between coats. When the surface is completely dry, sand with P320-grit. Use a stearated paper, like Norton's 3X, which has a soapy coating that resists clumping and clogging.

Dry finish won't clog sandpaper. Sanding dry shellac will produce a fine powder. If the finish isn't quite dry, the sandpaper will clog almost immediately.

A heavier cut builds faster. For the second and third coats, brush with a 1½-lb. cut. Heavier cuts get tacky soon after they're applied, so work quickly.

Eliminate drips. Use a fresh razor like a miniature card scraper to level drips and other imperfections. Don't bear down; instead, take multiple light passes until the drip is flush with the rest of the surface.

work toward your body. Use long, continuous strokes, overlapping them by ¼ in.

If you miss a spot or leave a drip, don't go back and touch it up—overworking it will leave deep brush marks that have to be sanded out. In two hours, sand with P320-grit to knock down the raised grain. Don't use alcohol to remove dust after sanding shellac because it will reactivate the finish. Use a tack cloth or compressed air instead.

Follow up with a rubdown. After making repairs, rub everything down thoroughly with a maroon abrasive pad (equivalent to 000 "extrafine" steel wool).

Finish with a 1-lb. cut. For the final coat, go back to the thinner, 1-lb. cut. It has longer open time, so it flows and "self-levels" a little better, minimizing brush marks.

Heavier coats build faster

The second and third coats—at a 1½-lb. cut—can be applied generously, in the same fashion as the first. Heavier cuts get tacky almost as soon as they're applied, so work quickly to avoid brush marks.

You can apply your third coat two hours after the second coat, then let everything dry overnight. The finish will appear very glossy, but don't sweat—you're not done.

Finish the finish

Before the final coat, it's time to address any drips or imperfections. Use a fresh razor like a card scraper to knock down drips, then rub out all surfaces with a maroon abrasive pad for an even matte sheen. Use the 1-lb. cut for the final coat, and let everything dry overnight.

For the final rubout, use superfine (0000) steel wool to knock down the sheen. If you want to add a coat of oil-based varnish for extra durability, now's the time. Apply paste wax with a soft cotton T-shirt rag, then buff it off for a deep, satiny finish.

Knock off the gloss. For the final rubout, use 0000 "superfine" steel wool to transform shellac's naturally glossy sheen into a uniform matte surface.

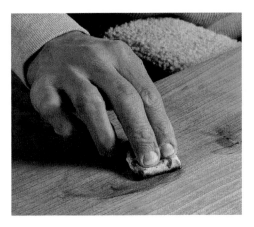

Wax on. Paste wax is the key to this satiny finish; use a soft T-shirt rag to distribute a very thin layer of wax across the surface.

Wax off. When the wax has hazed over, use a fresh cotton rag to remove it, working in a brisk, circular motion.

Fast Shellac Finish

MICHAEL PEKOVICH

hellac is a finish that a lot of woodworkers shy away from. If you've ever tried to brush it on straight from the can, you probably didn't like it very much. And if you've read an article on the fine art of French polishing, you're forgiven if you were left feeling a little intimidated.

The truth is that shellac is a great fast-drying finish that's easy to apply and perfect for small projects and last-minute gifts. It dries quickly between coats and lets you build up the finish gradually so you can really dial in the sheen you're looking for. I have a very simple technique that yields a nice satin finish that's friendly to the touch in about 30 minutes.

Thin the shellac for easy application. A one-to-one ratio of SealCoat, a dewaxed blond shellac, and denatured alcohol lets you wipe on thin coats that dry quickly.

One part alcohol

One part shellac

Start with a good base. The first coat, called the washcoat, seals the fibers and raises the grain. This coat will get sucked into the wood and dry quickly. After the washcoat is dry, use the highest-grit paper that you used for prep to knock down the raised grain.

Even, straight wipes. One of the benefits of this technique is the ability to build up the finish in thin coats. Apply the shellac in straight, slightly overlapping passes (top) and don't go over any areas again until the coat is dry. As your finish builds, smooth any rough spots or areas of raised grain with a light scuff of fine sandpaper (above).

Stop before the finish gets too thick. Pekovich applies coats until the surface is just a bit glossier than he wants in the finished product. This will ensure adequate protection without building too thick of a film finish.

The key to success is thin layers, but it all starts with surface preparation. Any mill marks, tearout, or sanding scratches will show up in the final finish, so getting a flat and smooth surface is a must. For open-pore woods like oak, sand to at least 400-grit; for closed-pore woods such as cherry and maple, sand to 600-grit.

Premixed must be remixed

One of the funky things about using shellac is that it's not ready to use straight from the can—it needs to be diluted. Undiluted, the shellac will be prone to runs and drips, and will take longer to dry. Diluting, or cutting, the shellac remedies these issues. Fortunately, getting the right mix ratio from canned

Prefinish as needed. Shellac dries fast, so you can finish parts without slowing down assembly. This means you can prefinish components like these dividers that would be hard to reach after glue-up.

shellac isn't difficult. I prefer SealCoat from Zinsser, a light-colored shellac with the wax removed. Wax occurs naturally in shellac, but removing it increases the clarity, durability, and moisture resistance of the finish as well as allowing other finishes to adhere to it. To use SealCoat, simply dilute it 1:1 with denatured alcohol.

Build the finish in thin coats

I wipe on the shellac with a clean cotton cloth. The diluted mixture will dry fast, so drips and runs shouldn't be a problem. Store the rag in a closed container to keep it from drying out and you can use it indefinitely.

No matter how smooth the surface was after sanding, it will probably feel rough after the first coat. The initial coat performed the important task of saturating the wood fibers and locking them in place. A quick sand with your final smoothing grit should return the smooth surface. With the fibers locked in

Smooth and wax in one step. The steel wool and wax combination levels any dust particles and produces a satin finish that's friendly to the touch. Wet the steel wool with some mineral spirits and then dip it into the wax. This will make it easier to apply a thin, even coat (top). Once the wax has dried, buff out the piece with a clean cotton rag (above).

place, the surface should stay fairly smooth through the rest of the finishing process.

Shellac is a solvent-based finish, which means wiping on a coat will partially dissolve the coats you've already applied. Don't wipe back and forth over wet surfaces or you'll run the risk of lifting off the finish as you're trying to build it up. Instead, wipe it on using straight, slightly overlapping coats, and wait for the surface to dry before applying additional coats. This might sound time consuming, but it's not. By the time you finish coating all the surfaces of a project, the first surfaces should be dry enough for the next coat. After three or four coats, the finish will stay sticky longer and dry more slowly. At this point, hold up for 10 minutes or so, which should be enough time for the finish to cure.

Before continuing, check for rough areas from raised grain or dust, and scuff-sand these spots with fine sandpaper as necessary. After another coat or two, you should be close to having enough finish on the project. Even though I'm aiming for a satin finish, I apply enough coats that it's slightly glossier than I'd like. The finish at this point might be a little streaky or have a slightly uneven shine, but that's OK. The last step will even everything out.

Finish with steel wool and wax

The final step is to rub out the finish by applying paste wax with fine steel wool. This should remove any roughness, but if you find any problem areas, hit them with 600-grit sandpaper. To make the wax easier to apply, dip the steel wool in mineral spirits first. This will dilute the wax for smoother application. Finally, buff the surface with a clean rag.

French Polishing Demystified

VIJAY VELJI

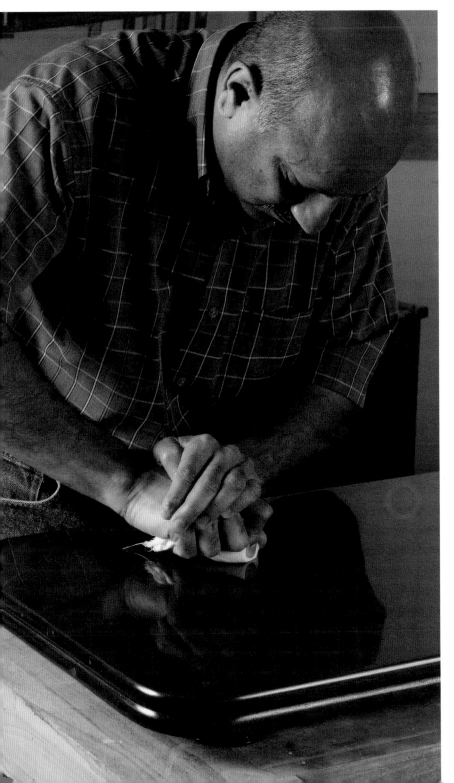

When I was growing up in Calcutta, India, my family's apartment had a clear view of a workshop that made high-end cabinets for radios. Standing there, I could watch the master craftsman make a carcase, veneer it, and finally finish it. For the latter, he used a curious circular motion with his hand that produced a most gleaming finish. Over time I talked to him about his technique, called French polishing, and after I had made a few pieces of furniture, I decided to try it myself.

In the years since, I've spent many hours reading articles about this mysterious finish, but practice was the key to getting the method correct. I will guide you through the process, from prepping the surface to filling the grain, from applying the shellac in very thin coats to giving the surface that final mirror shine. No other finish can match the clarity and depth of French polishing or the way it reveals a wood's beauty. There are no deep secrets to this finish, but there are some tips you need to know.

Careful sanding lays the foundation

Whether you are refinishing a piece, as with this card table, or finishing a new piece, the steps are the same. To start, the surface has to be dead flat with a uniform scratch pattern, because any irregularities will be magnified after the shellac is applied. Start sanding with P100-grit paper and work your way up

FRENCH POLISHING STEP-BY-STEP

Fill the grain

Build the finish

Bring out the shine

Don't forget the details

to P320-grit. You can use a random-orbit sander until the last grit, which must be done by hand using a cork-faced block, sanding with the grain. There are no shortcuts, so take your time.

You can French polish both flat and curved surfaces, but you can't get a polishing pad into inside corners. Because this piece is already assembled, I'll be brushing shellac on the inside corners of the base. However, it is perfectly possible on a new piece to polish the components first and then carefully assemble them. The only exceptions are small areas such as molding or trim.

Use fresh flakes

The best shellac for French polishing is dewaxed orange, garnet, beige, super blond, or platina flakes. Always use dewaxed shellac when finishing new or restoring old furniture. It is the wax in the shellac that gives rise to poor water resistance. Decanting seedlac or machine-made shellac can never get rid of enough wax, so use dewaxed varieties that have a wax content of 0.2% to 0.5%. Even in flake form, shellac has a shelf life of only two to three years, so don't use flakes you picked up at a tag sale. Also don't use premixed shellac sold in cans for French polishing, as the additives that extend its shelf life make it hard to pad on very thin coats.

Open-grained wood must be filled

To achieve a mirror-like finish, the polished surface must remain perfectly smooth. Because shellac shrinks over time, if you try to use it to fill wood pores, eventually the pore structure will reappear on the surface. On close-grained species such as cherry or maple, grain filling may not be necessary, but on open-grained woods like walnut and mahogany it certainly is. Use superfine

Fill the grain. Before being polished, open-pored wood must be filled with a mixture of shellac and pumice. Applying the mixture with a pad is good practice for later steps.

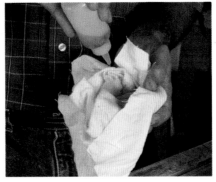

Pounce the pumice. Pour some superfine 4F pumice into a cotton bag and then knock the bag at even intervals on the workpiece.

Prepare the pad. The pad consists of a cotton batting core inside a linen covering. Dampen the core with very dilute shellac.

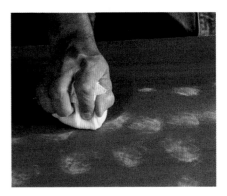

Fill the grain. Force the pumice into the wood's pores using a circular motion. Sprinkle on more pumice until the pores are filled.

Check your progress. To see if all the pores have been filled, check the surface against a raking light. You can also lightly run your fingernail across the grain. A smooth slide indicates that the pores are full.

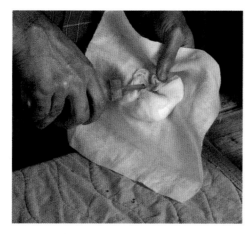

Build the finish. This is the heart of French polishing: padding on multiple layers of shellac. The thin layers dry so fast that you can build up a deep, smooth finish in one session, without stopping. To begin, start at the core. The second pad has a cheesecloth core and a linen cover. Dampen the core with alcohol and shellac.

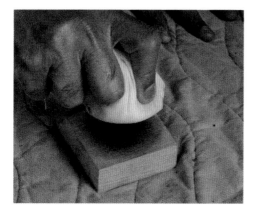

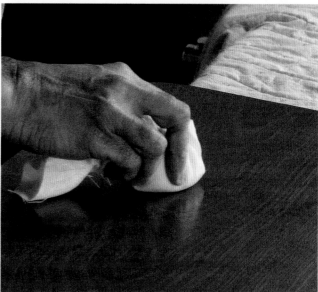

Knock it flat. After charging the pad, press it onto a scrap of wood to form a flat, wrinkle-free surface that will contact the workpiece.

4F pumice, a white volcanic rock. Sprinkle the pumice with a simple cotton bag made from a roughly 8-in. square of T-shirt material held together with a rubber band.

Make two pads—You will force the pumice into the pores with the first of two pads, so take a moment to create these tools. Take an 8-in.-square piece of linen and a ball of cotton batting that fits in your palm (see the center photo on p. 113). Place the ball on

Apply the shellac and raise the shine. Move the pad across the surface in a circular motion (top). You can employ a figure-eight pattern both along and across the grain, covering the entire surface of the wood. The shellac builds surprisingly quickly (above). Never stop the pad on the surface, as this will leave a mark.

Three Ways to Deal with a Sticky Pad

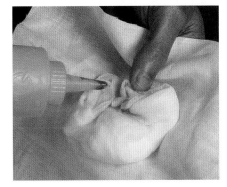

Recharge the pad with just alcohol. When the pad becomes sticky, try dampening the core with alcohol alone.

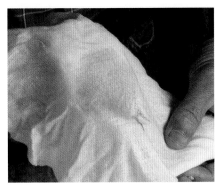

Move the core. If shellac starts to build up on the outside of the pad, it is more likely to stick. Move to a clean part of the linen.

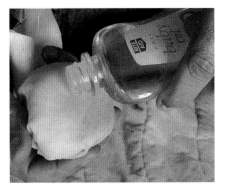

A little oil. Apply a drop of mineral oil to the pad. You will remove the oil from the workpiece later, so use as little as possible.

the linen, grasp the four corners of the linen, bring them together, and twist them tightly over the ball to form a pad. The second pad, used later, is almost identical but has a cheesecloth core. All three materials can be found at fabric stores.

Open the first pad and dampen the core with alcohol and a 1-lb. cut of shellac in roughly a 10:1 ratio, working it into the batting. Close the pad and sprinkle some pumice on the wood. Now work the pad with firm pressure in a circular pattern mostly across the grain. The pumice soon takes on the color of the wood. Avoid working with the grain because that will remove the pumice that has been packed into the pores.

The tiny amount of shellac is enough to create a kind of mastic that will glue the pumice in the pores. If you add too much shellac and the pad becomes sticky, simply add more alcohol. Grain filling is hard work, so take frequent breaks and try not to leave obvious swirls of the sawdust and pumice mixture on the surface. Recharge the pad

with alcohol and shellac and sprinkle more pumice as required. Once you are satisfied, lightly run your fingernail across the grain. A smooth slide indicates that the pores are full. Add a 1-lb. cut of shellac on the outside of the pad and lightly coat the surface. Let it dry for at least four hours.

Slightly wet the surface with water and lightly sand in a circular pattern using 1,500-grit wet-or-dry sandpaper. Dry sanding would create heat, melt the shellac, and clog the sandpaper, causing uneven sanding. Run your palm on the surface to determine if it is smooth and flat. Remove the residue with a clean cloth.

Thin coats dry almost instantly

To get a mirror surface, the finish has to be perfectly smooth. Any waves or ridges will scatter the light rays. The easiest way to build a smooth finish is to apply very thin layers using a 1-lb. cut of shellac. With experience, you can move toward a 2-lb. cut.

How to Handle Small Surfaces

1. Brush tight spots. Use an artist's brush to apply shellac to inside corners that a pad can't reach.

2. Blend the surface. Immediately after brushing on shellac, use the pad to feather the wet edge into the rest of the surface.

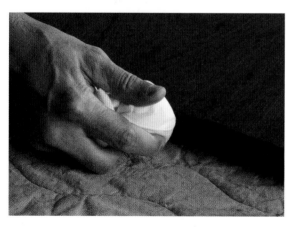

3. Don't forget the edges. Only the top surface needs to be grain filled and fully French polished, but you can use the pad to apply shellac to the rest of the workpiece while bodying the top.

The process of applying the shellac is known as bodying. Switch to the second pad. Dampen the cheesecloth core slightly with alcohol, then work in an equal mixture of alcohol and a 1-lb. cut of shellac. Twist the linen around the core and flatten the pad on a scrap of wood. Move the pad in a small circular pattern over the surface. Look for a faint glow of shellac seeping through the linen as it flows out of the core. As well as the circular pattern, you can employ a figure-eight pattern both along and across the grain, covering the entire surface of the wood. As the pad dries out, open it and add equal amounts of shellac and alcohol to the core. Never add shellac from the outside of the pad because the shellac must flow in a controlled manner from the core.

As the shellac builds up in the pad, it may get sticky. This can cause the linen fibers to separate and end up in the finish. There are three ways to deal with a sticky pad: Recharge the core with alcohol. If you see any accumulation of shellac on the linen cover, move the inner core to a new part of the linen. As a last resort, add a drop of mineral oil on the outside of the pad. Any oil added now has to be removed at the later stage of burnishing, so use it sparingly. Luckily, fresh flakes usually don't need much oil.

Bodying is the most time-consuming part of French polishing. You can do it in one long stretch or spread it out over several days. I can't give you a rule on how much shellac to apply; a grain-filled, open-pored wood will usually require more than a close-pored wood. To determine if the bodying process is complete, look at the surface from an angle against the light. If you see any pores of wood grain, you have more work to do. The initial bodying process is complete once you've laid a flat and even layer of shellac over the entire surface.

Now burnish everything. After letting the surface dry overnight, check to see if the shellac has shrunk into the wood pores and more shellac needs to be applied (above). Then use a barely dampened pad to burnish the shellac to a mirror finish (right). At the same time, the pad removes any oil that was used when building the layers of finish.

Let it dry overnight. The next morning, because shellac shrinks as it dries, you may see some areas that require more work. Continue with the bodying process, but if you have been using one of the darker grades of shellac, switch to super blond or platina. These grades have the best resistance to moisture.

Once the pores are filled with shellac and the surface looks perfectly smooth again, start using alcohol alone to get rid of all the shellac from the core as well as the linen. Again let the piece sit overnight to double-check that shellac shrinkage doesn't reveal any more pores.

Burnish the surface for that mirror finish

Burnishing is where you evenly stretch the shellac and remove any oil used when bodying the finish. You can use the same pad, but if the linen cover looks thin and worn, replace the whole pad.

Burnishing is hard labor because pressure must be applied on a pad that is almost dry to the touch. If you are using an old pad, wet just the core with alcohol. Use a little more alcohol to wet the core of a new pad. Move the pad with the grain and sometimes in small circular patterns, always applying pressure and always moving. If you stop, the pad will stick and mar the surface. If this happens, try burnishing away the blemish; if this doesn't work, you will have to apply more shellac. If the pad gets too dry, add alcohol very sparingly.

Working this way will give you the mirror finish you have heard about. By the way, you do not have to apply a layer of wax because the shellac is hard and durable enough to stand on its own merits for a long time.

Antique Finish That Holds Nothing Back

PETER GEDRYS

Building any reproduction involves a great deal of time, effort, and expense, so when the last drawer is fitted you might be tempted to apply the finish as quickly as possible. After all, you've put a lot of hours into the piece and you just want it done. You might also be afraid that anything more than the simplest of finishes could ruin all your hard work.

However, just as your cabinetmaking skills have progressed from butt joints and basic boxes to dovetails and desks, so you should expand your finishing horizons beyond wiping on oil. Finishing is no harder than woodworking, just a different skill set.

I'll show you how to imitate a century or three of use and age to form that unique surface known as a patina. It involves choosing and using dyes, filling open-pored woods, adding depth to the color with a glaze, applying a clear topcoat, and using surface tricks to age a piece. Unquestionably, it takes longer than applying a wipe-on varnish, but when you are already months into an heirloom project, what's a couple of weeks more? Give your reproduction the finish it deserves, one that creates a wow factor each time someone sets eyes on it.

Practice and experiment—but not on the piece

Start by looking at finishes that you'd like to replicate. This is similar to getting ideas when you design a piece. Look at books, magazines,

auction catalogs, and websites and see what colors and finishes please you.

Once you've settled on the look you want, see where you're starting from. Take the sample boards from each part of the piece and wet them with a solvent to see the base color of the wood. You can use alcohol for a quick preview or slower-drying mineral spirits for a longer study.

On this Federal desk, built by former *Fine Woodworking* Managing Editor Mark Schofield, I wanted to darken the main veneer, which had a strong, pinkish-red base to it. On the first sample board, I applied Chippendale Red Brown dye (all the dye powders I used are water-soluble) and when it dried, applied several coats of shellac. This left the wood darker but still with too much red, so then I used Georgian Brown Mahogany instead. This cool, greenish-brown dye neutralized the base red to a more pleasing brown.

I also experimented on samples of the tiger maple on the legs and the bird's-eye maple drawer fronts before settling on a combination of colors.

Sand the whole piece but seal it selectively

It's better to spend a little extra time fine-tuning the surface than to discover flaws after you start applying the dyes.

Use the Five Classic Steps

You'll need five fundamental finishing techniques to create a period patina, but none is very hard, and each is worth learning. You can use them in different combinations to create an infinite variety of effects on many styles of furniture.

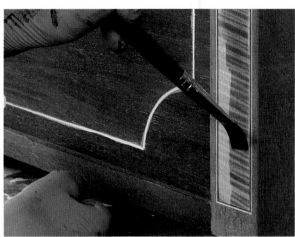

1. Dye the wood. Antiques often have deep, dark colors. Tiger maple goes a rich golden brown, and to imitate this look, begin by dyeing the bare wood.

2. Fill the grain. When using any film finish on open-grained wood, you should fill the grain. While antiques may have some visible pore structure in the finish, there are no deep voids.

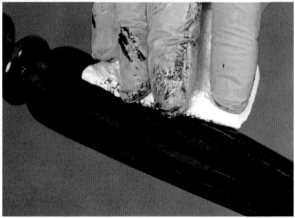

3. Glaze selectively. To simulate wear and tear in the carved areas, apply a translucent color over a sealed surface, leaving more in the recesses.

4. Lay down a topcoat. Shellac is the traditional clear finish for period pieces. Padding it on greatly reduces the need to rub out the final coat.

5. Leave wax in the corners. Dark wax applied in crevices and corners imitates centuries of dust and dirt. Don't go overboard; a little wax is all it takes to fool the eye.

Seal selective areas before you dye. Dyes add decades of darkening but before applying any, washcoat end grain with a thin coat of shellac to prevent it from absorbing too much dye.

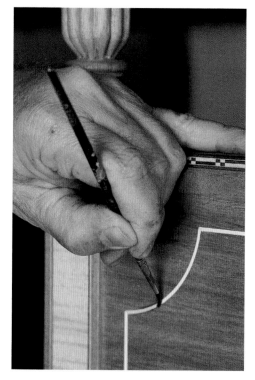

Protect light-colored woods. To prevent the holly stringing from being discolored, use a narrow brush to seal it with a thin coat of varnish.

TIP You don't have to dye every species of wood in a particular piece, but for each one you do dye, use a sample board of the same species to select the dye colors.

After a final hand-sanding with P180-grit paper, I remove the dust and wipe the surface with alcohol. This reveals any areas with glue residue that require a little extra sanding.

Once I'm satisfied that all is well with the surface, I clean it well, blowing out the pores with compressed air, vacuuming it, and giving it a good wipe-down with clean, dry, lint-free cloths.

If you have the steady hand of a marksman, you can try to apply the dye up to but not onto the holly stringing and banding. For the rest of us, it's safer to isolate the areas you don't want to dye. I've found that masking tape, even when burnished, isn't effective because the thin dye seeps under the edge.

Instead, I dilute varnish to a water-like viscosity and use it to seal the stringing and banding. Apply it with a small sable artist's brush. You should be able to go 8 in. to 10 in. before having to reload your brush. When you begin again, land the brush gently like a plane, overlapping the previous stroke about an inch or so. This ensures you don't miss a spot on the stringing.

It is a good idea to practice with denatured alcohol before trying it with varnish. One trick I have for areas close to an edge is to use

Apply the Dye

The whole surface of this desk was dyed, with the exception of the inlays, which were presealed to resist the dyes and retain their color. Dye numbers refer to W.D. Lockwood's catalog.

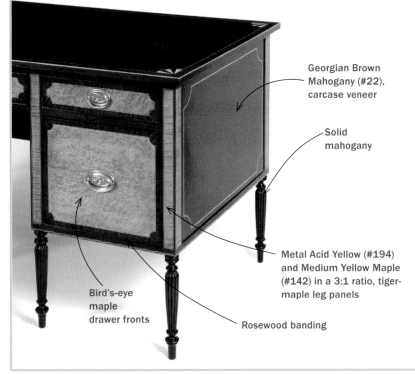

Georgian Brown Mahogany (#22), carcase veneer

Solid mahogany

Bird's-eye maple drawer fronts

Metal Acid Yellow (#194) and Medium Yellow Maple (#142) in a 3:1 ratio, tiger-maple leg panels

Rosewood banding

Apply the dye. A flat artist's brush works well in confined areas (above), while a folded paper towel covers large areas quickly (right). Try to even out the color while the dye is wet.

my baby finger as a kind of guide fence. Don't be in a rush: With all the stringing on the base, drawers, and top of this desk, this step took me the better part of a day. It is exacting work but no more so than laying in the stringing or the fans in the first place.

Let the coloring begin

Once the inlays and stringing are isolated, apply the dye. For confined spaces, I use a #20 bright artist's brush, but for larger areas I use a non-embossed industrial paper towel folded over a couple of times. I like these because they hold a lot of dye, flatten out nicely to a sharp edge, and give me a great deal of control. Even though the inlays are

coated, try to avoid running the dye over them. You know the old saying: An ounce of prevention is worth a pound of cure.

I used the same yellow dye on the rosewood that I used on the maple because it creates color harmony to the eye. Later, I'll tweak the rosewood's appearance by glazing it (see p. 125). After I've dyed the whole piece, I let it dry overnight and then look for areas either missed or dyed by mistake. You can try sanding any dyed sections of holly, but if this doesn't work, apply a matching gouache (an opaque artist's watercolor) with a #2 artist's brush.

I next rub the surface very sparingly with boiled linseed oil. I used less than 3 oz. for

Sand away mistakes. If dye strays onto the wrong wood, wrap medium-grit sandpaper around a credit card and sand that section. A straightedge helps guide the sandpaper.

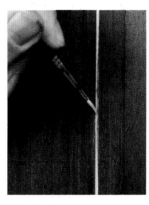

Pigment trumps dye. If you can't sand away errant dye, use opaque artist's watercolors to cover the affected area.

the whole desk, but this is enough to set the dye in the wood. After the oil has cured overnight, I apply a 1½ -lb. cut of blond, dewaxed shellac. This can be done by brush, pad, or spray and serves to isolate the base colors you just applied from the color in the grain filler applied next.

Finish alone can't fill open-pored wood

A formal finish needs to have a flat surface. If you apply a film finish to open-pored wood, it will leave the surface with a hungry look. Instead you need to apply a grain or paste filler. You can get paste filler already colored, but I prefer to tint my own to get a better

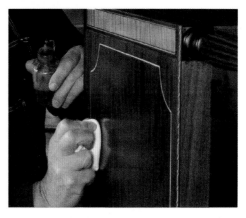

Seal in the dye. Before filling the grain, seal the dyed wood with a coat of dewaxed shellac. Otherwise, the filler will discolor the surface.

Stains replace dyes. If you discover a section that wasn't dyed after you've sealed the surface, use a pigment stain to apply color over the sealer. Two choices are gel stains or universal tints. If using the latter, mix it with a binder such as shellac.

match with the wood. I use an oil-based filler from Sherwin-Williams®, which in this case I tinted with raw umber and a dash of black artist's oils.

Paste filler requires thorough mixing to be effective. Once I have it colored, I'll pour it into a cup lined with cheesecloth folded over a couple of times. Then I gather the

cheesecloth at the top and pull down on it, forcing the paste filler through it. This ensures my filler is lump free and the color is well incorporated.

You can apply the filler with a brush or a plastic blade. The pores on this wood are large and pronounced, so I used a short-bristle brush to force the filler in. Be sure to apply filler in manageable sections; otherwise, it will become very difficult to remove as it dries. Start with an area of a couple of square feet.

Although burlap is often recommended for removal, I've never liked it. I scrape off most of the excess with a plastic spreader going at 45° or perpendicular to the grain to avoid pulling filler out of the pores. Then I use a white abrasive pad to erase any filler that remains on the surface. These work great, and I can use a clogged pad to apply filler to carved areas such as the reeded legs. I simply rub the pad around the leg a few times, and then come back with a sharpened dowel to remove any filler from the groove between each reed. After letting the filler cure for five to six hours, I wipe all the

Use filler on open-pored woods. Gedrys likes to use uncolored, oil-based grain filler that he tints using artist's oils.

Filter the filler. After adding the colors, squeeze the filler through layers of cheesecloth to mix in the color and remove lumps.

Pack the pores. Use an old paintbrush to force the filler into the pores. Let the filler cure for a few minutes and then pull a plastic squeegee across the surface perpendicular to the grain to remove the excess.

Clean the surface. A white abrasive pad does a great job scrubbing any remaining filler from the surface while leaving the pores filled. Don't wait or the filler will harden on the surface.

Fill grain on carvings, too. A clever way to fill the pores on carvings is to take a pad used to remove surplus filler from flat surfaces, and rub it over the carving, working it into the recesses, too.

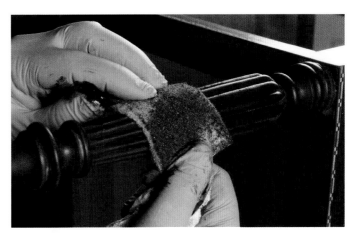

surfaces with a clean cloth dampened with mineral spirits and let the piece sit overnight.

Don't be surprised if very open-pored wood requires a second round of filling. Don't skimp on this step or you'll find yourself trying to compensate later with the clear coat.

Once the pores are filled, let the piece dry for a few days and then seal the surface with a 2-lb. cut of dewaxed shellac in preparation for glazing.

Glazing adds depth to the color

If you study antiques closely, one of their major differences with modern pieces is the subtle darkening found on some surfaces, particularly on carvings. The best way to imitate this combination of buildup in the recesses and greater wear on the high points is by a technique known as glazing.

Glaze is a translucent color applied over a sealed surface. It is a versatile tool in the finisher's arsenal because it is very forgiving. If you don't like what you see, simply wipe it off before it dries.

Seal again, then glaze. Glazing simulates wear and tear. Tint an oil-based glazing stain to the desired color or use diluted asphaltum. Apply it to the sealed surface.

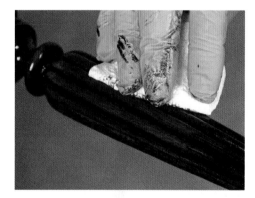

Wipe the high points. Use a paper towel to remove the glaze from the prominent surfaces, which are lighter on antiques.

Blend the transition. Use a dry brush to soften the line between the glazed and unglazed areas.

In this case, I used asphaltum as my glaze. A black, naturally occurring, tar-like substance, it mixes well with mineral spirits to produce a rich golden brown. It's easy to adjust the color strength by adding more asphaltum to the thinner. During application, less is more. Light applications read better to the eye than thick ones. Remember, you can always add more glaze if required.

I apply the glaze with a pad, paper towel, or brush on flat areas such as the rosewood banding, but for carved areas I use an artist's fan brush to reach into the recesses. This brush has short, stiff bristles that allow me to quickly apply a thin coat of glaze to, in this case, the reeded legs. Next, use a paper towel to remove the glaze from the high points. To feather out or blend the resulting unnaturally sharp line between the glazed and unglazed areas, gently go over the surface with a dry artist's brush to give the glaze a harmonious appearance.

Color with shellac. It is fine to use one type of finish such as shellac on the base and add a more durable one such as varnish or lacquer to the top. If you choose shellac as your finish coat, tweak the final appearance by selecting a color ranging from super blond to garnet.

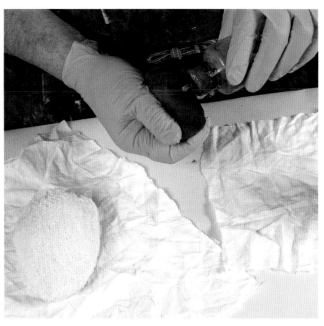

Make your pad. Gedrys uses a cheesecloth core inside a linen wrapping. Add the shellac to the core for a consistent release onto the workpiece.

You have a choice of clear finishes

Set the piece aside for a few days to dry well before you apply the clear topcoat. You have a number of choices based on the application method you feel most comfortable with and the amount of use the finished piece will receive. It is perfectly fine to use two different types of finish on a single piece. On this desk, I padded shellac onto the base and used wiping varnish on the top for extra protection, but you could also brush on either of those finishes or spray the top with lacquer.

On the base, after I sand the sealer coat well on the non-glazed areas with P320-grit paper, I pad on shellac. I use an identical pad to one used for French polishing and basically the same technique. This includes the same circular and figure-8 patterns, but I

Build the finish. The advantage to padding on shellac over brushing is that you end up with a smooth finish (devoid of brush marks) that doesn't need rubbing out.

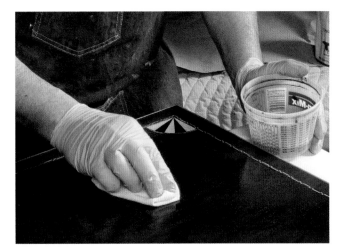

A durable top. To give the desktop extra protection, Gedrys wiped on some thinned varnish over the shellac sealer.

Wax the recesses. To imitate dust buildup, begin by using an old artist's brush to push clear paste wax into the recesses of carvings.

lay down slightly thicker coats and finish by going with the grain. The advantage of the pad is that it doesn't leave any brush marks and the surface is refined during application, eliminating the need to rub it out afterward. Take the time to practice this technique. You'll be happy you did.

On the top, I sealed the surface with a 2-lb. cut of dewaxed shellac and then wiped on four coats of Behlen's Rockhard™ Table Top Varnish, thinning the varnish by about 40% with mineral spirits. This is enough protection for a desktop, but dining tables would be safer with three brushed-on coats, thinning the finish by 10% to 15% and sanding between each coat.

The finishing touches

When all the finish coats were done, I set the desk aside for a week prior to any rubbing out. This also gave me the chance to look at the piece and to consider whether it needed any more aging.

There are some subtle surface techniques done with a little wax and rottenstone that imitate the buildup of dust, grime, and polish. Whether you wax the whole piece

Add your dust. Brush rottenstone onto the freshly waxed areas. Rottenstone's pale blue/gray cast mimics dust well.

Complete the effect. After 20 minutes, use a piece of folded newspaper to remove most of the rottenstone, but leave traces deep in the recesses.

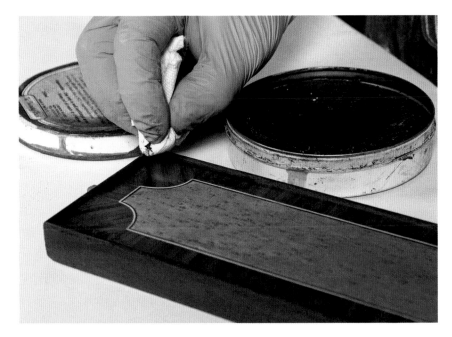

Dark wax in the corners. Wipe on some dark wax, letting it build up in the corners to imitate antiques.

Patinating pulls. To add contrast to the antique-finish pulls, first use brass polish to give shine to the wear points, then rub some dark wax into the recesses. Finally, buff the whole surface with a clean cotton cloth.

is entirely optional. In this case, it doesn't affect the look of the piece but it does give a uniquely attractive quality to the touch.

The beauty of this finish is its visual depth. Once you've tried it, experiment with some of the steps and colorants to create your own patinas.

Sources

Dyes
www.wdlockwood.com

Shellac flakes, SealCoat shellac, white pads, grain filler and plastic spreaders, natural or tinted glazes, Behlen's Rockhard Table Top Varnish, paste wax, rottenstone, patinating wax
www.woodworker.com

Artist's brushes, artist's oil colors, asphaltum
www.dickblick.com
www.winsornewton.com

Lather Up

REED HANSULD

I first learned of using soap flakes as a wood finish from a Danish furniture maker who said it was traditionally used in Denmark on everything from chairs and tables to case goods and floors. I was skeptical, but when I saw it on a cabinet he'd made I had to try it. Four years later, it's my finish of choice. With its low sheen, this in-the-grain finish has a muted beauty that enhances the look of wood being wood. And it's smoother to the touch than any finish I've encountered.

A soap finish won't take abuse like varnish or epoxy, but it's simple to renew and a pleasure to apply. It is nothing more than soap flakes and water, so it's as environmentally friendly a wood finish as you'll find—zero VOCs (volatile organic compounds). You won't need a respirator, glasses, or gloves; there's nothing toxic to avoid and nothing dangerous to dispose of. And it's quicker to apply than most wipe-on finishes.

A soap finish is well suited for lighter-toned woods like white oak, ash, maple, and beech. Unlike oils and some waxes, soap won't produce an amber tone, so light woods look bright. It doesn't provide UV protection, so the wood will naturally darken over time. Soap isn't a good match for darker woods; it won't draw out the depth of grain and color in woods like walnut, cherry, or rosewood. Also, because of all the water involved, I'd hesitate to use it on a veneered piece.

Mix it up. A small handful of pure soap flakes and ½ cup of very hot water make enough froth for one coat of finish on a small project like the chair below. Soap for multiple coats can be mixed at once and used over the course of a day.

Whip it. With a fork or spoon chucked in a drill, whisk the mixture until it is the consistency of whipped cream, stiff enough to hold peaks. An immersion blender also works.

Clean Finish for Light Woods

Traditional in Scandinavia, the simple-to-apply soap flake finish brings a bony whiteness to light-colored woods, producing a low-level sheen and a satiny smooth surface.

Start with water. Before applying the soap froth, raise the grain by rubbing the workpiece with water, then sand with 220-grit paper.

Mix it up and slather it on

The process of mixing is incredibly simple: Add a handful of flakes to half a cup of hot water, and whir. Be sure the flakes are pure and unscented. I use Dri-Pak flakes (www.msodistributing.com). Whisk for a few minutes with a fork or spoon in a hand drill—or with an immersion blender— until you get a thick, dense froth. Like whipped cream, it should hold peaks and never be runny. And there should be no undissolved flakes.

Apply the froth with a clean cotton rag, going over the workpiece thoroughly and soaping the parts more than once per coat. Then go over the piece with a fresh rag, removing excess suds and really buffing the finish into the wood. At this point, I rinse out the buffing rag and hang it to dry with

the rinsed application rag. Both can be reused for the next coat.

In an hour or so, when the work is dry, do a light sanding. After the first coat or two, I use 220-grit, and after subsequent coats, I work upward to 600-grit or higher. I have found a minimum of three coats are required, and I've done as many as 10—all of which can be done in a single day as long as you leave adequate drying time between coats. The following day I buff it with a white fine abrasive pad (Norton Bear-tex® hand pads) and the finish is complete.

The finish should be renewed every year or so. Stains can be spot-treated by rubbing the stained area with very hot water and recoating with soap froth. If the stain persists, scrape or sand through to clean wood before applying the froth.

Spread the froth. Use a clean cotton cloth to spread the soap over the piece. Apply it over the whole surface several times per coat (1). Use a clean and dry rag to remove the froth and rub down the whole coat vigorously (2). When the coat is dry—in an hour or so—sand all surfaces (3). For early coats, use 220-grit paper; for later ones, progress up to 600-grit. Three to 10 coats make a good finish. The day after you've applied the finish, buff the workpiece with a very fine abrasive pad (4).

All about Wax

PETER GEDRYS

There is a quality to a wax topcoat that can't be matched by more durable, modern finishes. The soft sheen and tactile quality of a waxed surface just begs to be touched. Not only does a waxed surface look good and feel good, but it also helps protect the finish underneath.

Besides being a final coat on finished wood, wax has a number of other uses. It can serve as a minimal finish to maintain a wood's natural beauty, or it can give a just-made piece an antique look. Colored waxes can create special effects. Best of all, the tools are simple and the techniques are easy. Whatever your furniture-making ability, your projects will look and feel better after a proper waxing.

Wax polish finishes a finish

The most common use for wax is to apply it as the final layer of finish. It can go on top of any type of finish, from an in-the-wood couple of coats of oil to high-gloss, rubbed-out shellac. The wax helps to even out the sheen and adds a measure of protection that can be renewed easily. However, don't be in a rush to apply it: Almost all waxes contain solvents, which can damage a film finish that isn't fully cured. For most finishes, this means waiting a week, but wait at least a month before applying a paste wax to solvent-based lacquer.

For best results, use an applicator—
Using widely available but hard paste waxes, beginners tend to put on too much, then wonder why the surface smears when they try to buff it. The answer is to make a wax applicator.

Take some good, dense cheesecloth and fold it over. Place a small amount of wax on the middle of this pad. Gather up the edges and twist them to form a small knob that

Choose One Made for Furniture

In general, if the first use mentioned on the can is polishing wood floors, don't use the wax on furniture. It is likely to contain a high percentage of carnauba wax and is designed to be buffed with a mechanical floor buffer. You'll have a hard time buffing it by hand. Butcher's® Bowling Alley Wax and Minwax finishing wax fall into this category. However, these hard paste waxes can be used as a clear base for custom-coloring. In general, waxes designed for furniture are easier to use. They usually are softer in consistency (what I call a semi-paste wax) due to their higher percentage of solvent, which makes them easier to apply. I've had good results with Antiquax; Fiddes dries fast and has a low odor; Liberon's Black Bison goes on very smoothly but has a strong odor; Goddard's® has a pleasant lemon verbena scent.

Clear-Wax Basics

Although brands of wax vary greatly in price, they all draw from the same limited number of raw waxes and solvents. The best-known wax is beeswax. After the honeycomb has been melted and refined, it can be left dark or placed in the sun and bleached. Medium-soft, beeswax produces a medium-gloss finish.

The cheapest component is paraffin wax, derived from refining crude oil. Relatively soft and colorless, it serves as the base for many wax blends. Also obtained from petroleum is microcrystalline wax, a highly refined and expensive wax that has excellent resistance to water. It is favored by museums because of its neutral pH.

To offset paraffin wax's softness, manufacturers add harder waxes: Carnauba, obtained from scraping the leaves of a Brazilian palm tree, produces a very high shine but is also very hard to buff out when used alone; candelilla, obtained from the leaves of a Mexican plant, is much like carnauba but somewhat softer.

The speed at which a solvent evaporates will determine how long you have to wait before you can buff the wax. Traditionally, turpentine was used to dissolve beeswax, but its relative expense means this medium-paced solvent is rarely used in commercial waxes.

Mineral spirits is the most common solvent and can be formulated for slow or medium-paced evaporation. Faster-evaporating solvents include naphtha and toluene. I avoid toluene waxes such as Briwax® for a number of reasons. First, I dislike their strong odor; second, toluene is most likely to damage a finish that is not fully cured; third, I find they harden very fast, making them somewhat difficult to work with.

Raw waxes. Shown from left are beeswax, paraffin, and carnauba flakes.

Colored Wax

If you do one thing after reading this chapter, I hope you'll try using a dark wax. As this piece of walnut shows, a clear wax on a dark, open-pored wood can leave white residue in the pores. Even if the pores are filled, the clear wax can leave a slight haze on a dark surface.

Conversely, wax the same color or darker than the wood can enhance the appearance. See p. 141 for more detail and to learn how dark wax can be used to give an aged look.

You can buy wax in a range of wood tones, or you can take clear paste wax and color it yourself. You must first melt the wax, but because wax is flammable, never heat it over an open flame. Instead, place it in a container over heated water, a device known as a double boiler. Add artist's oils or universal colorants and mix them in thoroughly. Let the wax solidify before use.

Clear wax

Dark wax

Buy the right color. Find one that matches the wood and it won't show in pores and recesses.

Or color your own. If you need only a small amount of colored wax or you want an unusual color, melt some clear paste wax in a container over hot water, and then mix in artist's oil colors.

encloses the wax. As soon as you rub the surface, the wax will start coming through the cloth evenly and thinly. Although you can use softer semi-paste wax this way, you gain the most benefit when using harder paste waxes. For closed-pore, light-colored woods such as maple, I use a clear wax, but for open-pore woods such as oak or mahogany and darker closed-pore woods like cherry, I use a colored wax.

When you rub the surface, you will apply a very thin film of wax. The applicator prevents you from applying too much. I begin by applying the wax in circles, forcing it into any open pores, and then I give it a once-over with the grain to straighten everything out. If you run out of wax, don't apply more to the outside of the applicator; just unwrap it and replenish the inside. When finished, you can store the applicator inside the can of wax.

To get the best results, you must wait for the solvent to evaporate before you remove the excess wax and buff the surface. If you do this too soon, you'll either remove the wax or just move it around. If you wait too long, it becomes progressively harder to remove the surplus. Although the wax won't get hazy like car polish, it will change from glossy to dull. The time this takes varies by brand and atmospheric conditions, but 20 minutes is average.

Although using the applicator should prevent excess wax, I still rub the dried wax with a white nylon nonabrasive pad (www.woodworker.com). The open weave picks up any thicker patches or small lumps of wax. The final step is to buff the surface with a soft cloth like terrycloth, an old T-shirt, or even a paper towel. Rub the surface vigorously and turn the cloth frequently so that you burnish the wax rather than just redistribute it.

At this stage, if you find you simply can't get the surface to shine, you probably put on too much wax or let it harden for too long.

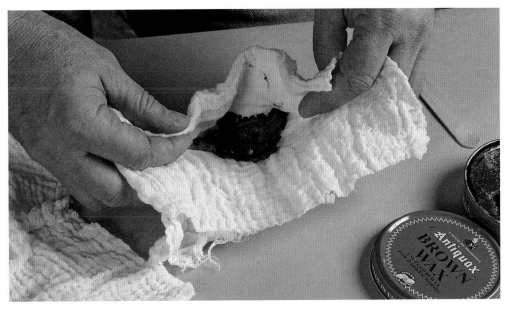

Create a wax applicator. Place some wax in the center of a double thickness of cheesecloth, gather the edges of the cloth together, and twist them closed.

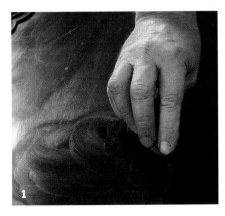

Gloss look. The cheesecloth applicator allows an even amount of wax to reach the wood. Apply the wax in a circular motion (1). Follow up by giving some light strokes with the grain (2). Before buffing, wipe the surface with a white nonabrasive pad; the open weave picks up any residue (3). Don't use a colored pad; many contain abrasives. To raise the shine, you can do the final buffing with a cotton cloth or a paper towel (4). Turn it frequently to keep removing surplus wax.

Satin sheen. You can combine rubbing out the finish and waxing it by using steel wool to apply the wax. Liberon's 0000 steel wool gives the most even scratch pattern (right). To avoid cross-grain scratches, rub the steel wool with the wax in the direction of the grain only (below).

Not just for shoes. You can buff wax with a brush. This works well in carved areas and produces a slightly lower shine than a cloth.

Rub the surface with a cloth dampened with mineral spirits to remove most of the wax. Wait an hour for the solvent to evaporate, and then reapply the wax more carefully.

Rub out the surface with wax—

If you prefer a medium luster, an option when waxing a cured finish such as shellac, varnish, or lacquer is to apply the wax with 0000 steel wool or a gray abrasive pad. This will reduce the sheen and soften the look. To better lubricate the steel wool, I use a softer semi-paste wax. To avoid cross-grain scratches, apply the wax with the grain only. It is easy to apply too much wax with this method, so you'll probably need to go over the wax once it has dried with clean steel wool or a white abrasive pad. When the wax has cured, buff the surface in the same way as previously described.

Waxing intricate shapes and carvings—

By highlighting areas that are proud and leaving recesses dull, wax can give carvings and moldings a more three-dimensional appearance. The softer the wax, the easier it is to work into the corners using either a cloth or a small stiff brush. When dry, a vigorous buffing with a dry and moderately stiff-bristle brush will yield good results.

Renewing a waxed surface—

When a waxed surface begins to look dull, try buffing to renew the sheen. If this doesn't do the trick, simply apply and buff another layer of wax in the same way as described earlier. When done correctly, the layers of wax are so thin you need have no concern about wax buildup.

If the surface becomes worn or dirty, wax can be removed with mineral spirits or one of the proprietary wax washes. If it is very grimy, use either 0000 steel wool or a gray

As a minimal finish.
For objects rarely touched and that don't need a protective finish, wipe on a single coat of shellac, sand when dry, and then wax and buff.

Pop the pores with colored wax. Open the pores by brushing the wood with a bronze or brass brush. After removing the dust with a vacuum or compressed air, apply a single coat of shellac.

A limed finish. Fill the pores with white liming wax, and then remove the surplus. Later add a coat of clear wax, or for a higher gloss, a coat of shellac.

Color wax with powders.
You can color clear wax by adding dry pigments or mica powders. Afterward, topcoat with either clear wax or shellac.

Dirt in the crevices. To give an aged appearance, apply softened paste wax into the nooks and crannies of carvings. Then tap in some rottenstone with a stiff-bristled brush (above). When the wax has dried, rub the area with crumpled newspaper to remove the bulk of the rottenstone, and then burnish the high points with a cloth (right). This leaves a line of gray similar to that found on antiques.

abrasive pad with solvent to loosen the wax. Wipe well with paper towels, and then rewax the surface.

Wax bare wood for a natural look

Wax also can be used on its own as a finish. It has the advantage of barely changing the natural color of the wood, just giving the surface a slightly higher sheen. The downside is that it gives minimal protection, but this is not a problem for objects such as picture frames that are subject to infrequent handling. As with waxing a finish, you need to match the wax color to the wood.

A variation on this is one of my favorite finishes. I seal the bare wood with a coat or two of a 1-lb. to 2-lb. cut of shellac, lightly sand it when dry, and then apply the wax. I've used it with great success on lightly used furniture and on architectural components such as paneling. The thin barrier of shellac barely changes the wood's appearance yet makes it smoother and less porous, allowing a more even luster. It also allows me to easily remove the wax at a later date, if required.

Colored wax gives a range of looks

Wax comes in a range of colors, from wood tones to specialty colors such as black and

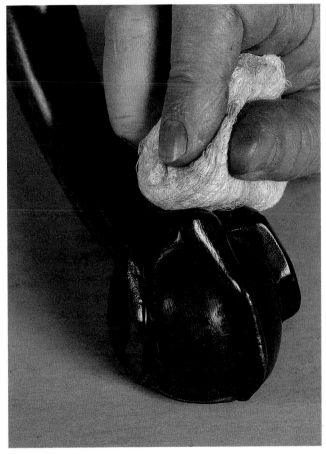

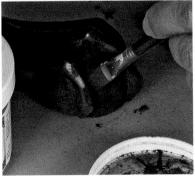

Simulate wax buildup. To replicate the dark recesses found on antiques, use dark wax in these areas (above), or apply dry pigments to freshly applied clear wax (left). When the wax is dry, burnish the high points with a cloth or a brush (right).

white. These colored waxes can be used either for decorative finishing or for replicating antiques.

A limed finish on white oak is the most famous decorative wax finish. First, open up the pores with a brass brush or a slightly stiffer bronze brush, then vacuum and blow out the pores thoroughly. Seal the surface with a thin coat of shellac, and then rub white wax well into the pores. Wipe off the excess and apply either a couple of coats of paste wax or, for a higher sheen, a coat of shellac. Other applications include adding colored pigments or mica powders to clear wax to color the pores.

If your taste runs more toward period than contemporary, wax can give furniture an aged appearance. Using wax a shade or

two darker than the wood will add accent lines around moldings and carvings. There are brown and black waxes sold as patinating waxes, but you can make your own or use dry pigment powders on top of a clear wax.

Don't use shoe polish. Many include silicone, which will play havoc with any film finish that you apply afterward.

Splash Color on Wood

SCOTT MCGLASSON

I've been splashing pigment on hardwood since my earliest days as a furniture maker. The instructor and old-timers at the vo-tech where I took night classes were aghast—I was skewering a sacred cow. But I kept it up, and now it's second nature to me. Color can do so much: It can energize a simple form, it can be edgy and iconoclastic, or it can be playful and add an element of surprise.

I worked my way through college as a painter and finisher on my way to an English degree. After a half dozen years working in education, I fell hard in love with woodworking and brought my painting and finishing knowledge to full-time furniture making.

I use a lot of different finishes to get color on my furniture. To achieve an opaque coating, I'll often spray pigmented lacquer. This is essentially like paint—the color is in the finish, not in the wood. I usually mix the colors myself using lacquer-based colorants, or TransTint®, a type of dye you can add to clear lacquer. But you can get pigmented lacquers professionally color-matched to just about anything. Lacquers need to be sprayed in a controlled environment with proper ventilation and good spraying skills, but they level like nothing else and are very durable.

Alternately, especially for white or black pieces, I'll use dyes or stains to color the wood directly, and then spray a clear or slightly tinted topcoat.

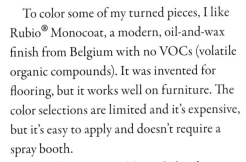

To color some of my turned pieces, I like Rubio® Monocoat, a modern, oil-and-wax finish from Belgium with no VOCs (volatile organic compounds). It was invented for flooring, but it works well on furniture. The color selections are limited and it's expensive, but it's easy to apply and doesn't require a spray booth.

Ash is the quiet workhorse behind showier species such as walnut in my painted furniture. Ash is dense, stable, and inexpensive. And with its deep, open grain, it is the perfect wood for opaque finishes. Light flickers across its distinctive texture, and even if the finish is thick, you'll always be aware there's wood underneath.

I use ash for the stack-laminated bodies of my turned pieces—stools, side tables, lamps,

and vessels. To prepare the turning blank, I'll glue up a stack of 8/4 disks of ash with one 4/4 disk of walnut at the top. Once I've turned the basic shape, I texture these pieces with grooves cut with a skew chisel. Random patterns of the open grain intersect with the controlled grooves, and when an opaque finish is applied, the appearance almost mimics the glazed surfaces of ceramics.

To apply color to one of my stools or benches, I'll flip the piece upside down on my finishing table and coat the entire underbody with black, blue, white, or red, leaving the top as a single plane of clear-coated walnut or cherry. When I turn it right side up, I gently ease the edge of the pigment with sandpaper and then spray a clear topcoat on the whole piece.

Some of my forms are riffs on traditional utilitarian furniture, taking influences from Scandinavian and rustic pieces. Adding splashes of color, while framing and enhancing the natural wood, brings my pieces to a modern place.

Better Than Paint

Whether in modern or traditional interiors, bookcases, built-ins, and cabinets sparkle when finished in a crisp, classic white. For maximum impact, this finish requires a very even application and a smooth finish, so it is typically sprayed on. But don't despair if you aren't set up to spray: I will show you how to get an off-the-gun-looking finish just by brushing and wiping. It will take longer than spraying, but the quality of this finish is well worth the wait.

While I could reach for oil-based or latex paint, I find that pigmented lacquer provides a superior look in terms of evenness and lack of residual brush marks. I prefer acrylic lacquers over nitrocellulose ones because

Right at home. You should design a built-in or entertainment center to match the design of the room, and a paint company can tint your lacquer to match, too.

145

TIP Why is this can upside-down? The manufacturer of Plastic Wood® intentionally inverts the label to encourage people to store the can lid-side-down. This old finisher's trick keeps air from leaking in and works well for any finish that tends to gel or harden in the can.

Prep the surface. A painted finish is far less forgiving of any surface defects than a clear finish is, so deal with these first. Clarke uses a knife blade to press wood filler into a knothole.

they are nonyellowing and retain brilliance better. I'm going to use a precatalyzed version here, which has better durability than a non-catalyzed lacquer and is easier to apply than a post-catalyzed lacquer. You can buy this type of lacquer from Sherwin-Williams or M.L. Campbell® paint stores and, if you like, they can tint it to match an existing color in your house.

A flawless finish needs perfect prep work

The best woods for painting are close-pored, such as poplar, maple, pine, or birch plywood. The high-solids primer that I'll use can fill medium-pored woods, but if you find yourself having to paint an open-pored wood such as oak, it would be best to apply an oil-based grain filler first.

Sand it flush. Use P150-grit paper wrapped around a cork-faced block or a sanding sponge to level the filled area.

Seal with shellac. To prevent resin from staining the finish in the future, seal all knots and sap pockets in pine with dewaxed shellac.

I begin to prep the surfaces by filling any imperfections with water- or solvent-based, natural-colored wood filler. Using a utility blade or flat spatula, I lay the wood filler into any indentations, leaving the filler slightly proud of the surface. For minor indentations (less than 1/16 in. deep and 3/16 in. wide), let the filler dry for one to two hours. Larger fills will require more drying time. Next, I sand the whole surface up to P180- or P220-grit. Wrap the sandpaper around a sanding block for a smooth, even surface. The block also ensures that the filled areas end up even with their surroundings.

Since this project is made from pine, I next apply a 2-lb. cut of shellac as a sealer on any knots or sap pockets. Without it, these areas can emit resin that eventually leaches through the finish. I apply a generous coat of dewaxed shellac to any knots, spreading it away from the center of each knot to blend into the unsealed surfaces. Let the shellac dry for about four hours, or until it is not tacky to the touch, then lightly dull the shellac with a purple abrasive pad, being careful not to cut through it.

Primer creates a smooth foundation

White lacquer primer is one of the big secrets. It builds a film that overcomes any imperfections too small to fill and it sands easily, leaving a flat, seamless surface devoid of grain texture, critical for a flawless finish. I work in a large, well-ventilated area; otherwise, I'd use a respirator.

I reduce the primer approximately 40% with the manufacturer's recommended solvent. This is slightly thinner than for spraying, but it makes the primer more workable and forgiving for a hand application. I prefer a large lacquer mop brush because of the amount of finish that it can carry, but a quality 2-in. natural-bristle

Prime First

A primer formulated for lacquer creates a flat, uniform-colored surface for the topcoat.

PRIMER RECIPE
60% primer, 40% thinner

Thinned for brushing.
To make it easier to brush, Clarke thins the primer with a lacquer thinner.

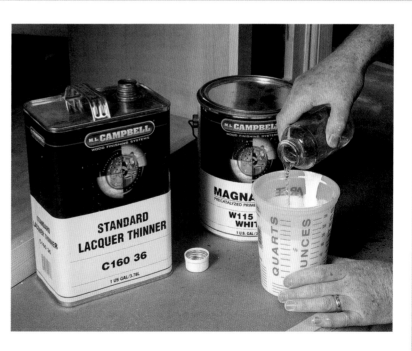

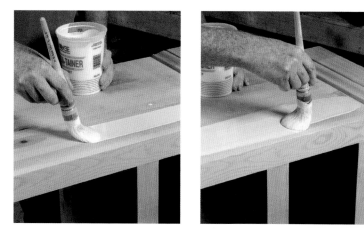

Best technique for flat areas: Unload, then spread. Load the brush and then lay down a thick strip of finish away from the edges (above left). Then come back and spread the finish out on both sides of the strip (above right). After reloading the brush, land it an inch or two from the wet area (right). Now it, too, can be spread out on both sides and will not create a ridge of excess finish.

Next coat. After the first coat is dry, apply the second coat of primer with the same technique but perpendicular to the first to reduce the buildup of brush marks.

Remove any flaws. Sand the surface and deal with any remaining problems before applying a third coat of primer. Lacquer primer is designed to be easily sanded. Wrap P220-grit paper around a block for flat areas, and hold it in your fingers for moldings.

flat brush is also a good choice. If possible, work on a horizontal surface, as this greatly reduces the chance of runs. Tip cabinets onto their sides and let one side dry before turning it over.

Brushing tips for primer and lacquer—Both the primer and topcoat are applied in the same way. I apply the first coat with the grain, starting a few inches from an

Remove all dust. After vacuuming the surface, lightly wipe it with a tack cloth to remove any remaining residue.

More flaws show up. The uniform appearance of the primer will probably reveal surface defects that were camouflaged by the natural wood. Fill and smooth them.

edge and applying the finish about half the length of a normal brush stroke. Then I go back and forth to spread it out on each side of the initial brush stroke. After recharging the brush, I land it about an inch or two away from the wet area, ensuring even coverage without a ridge of surplus finish.

On narrow moldings or details, I use a smaller #6 or #8 lacquer mop or a 1-in. natural-bristle flat brush. I let this whole first coat dry at least one to two hours, depending on temperature and humidity, and then

Deal with drips. If you can't catch a drip or run immediately, don't wipe the sticky surface. Let it dry, then shave it flush with a sharp knife. Clarke uses a utility blade.

evaluate the surface. Fill any imperfections that may have been missed in the initial filling; let the filler dry one to two hours (or longer for larger areas), and then block-sand the filled spots.

If the surface is fairly smooth (and didn't need more filling), you can skip sanding as long as you apply the next coat within 60 to 90 minutes. If you wait longer, or the surface is rough, sand it with P220-grit paper to smooth the surface and to create a mechanical bond with the next coat.

To apply the second primer coat, I work perpendicular to the grain, using the same technique. By applying coats alternately with and across the grain, you minimize a buildup of brush lines. If you are brushing a confined area, apply all the coats in the longer of the two directions. I allow this coat to dry for a minimum of two to four hours, depending on temperature and humidity, but overnight is fine, too.

I repeat the horizontal application for the third primer coat, let that dry for two to four hours, and then block-sand all the primed surfaces with P220-grit sandpaper. I use a vacuum with a brush attachment to carefully remove all the sanding dust. Wipe your hand across the surface. If it comes up white, gently use a tack cloth to remove any remaining dust.

Apply topcoats until you get the desired look

It's time to apply the tinted lacquer topcoats. Start by thinning the lacquer by approximately 30% with the manufacturer's recommended solvent and then add a further 10% in retarder. This gives the lacquer time to flow out before drying, minimizing brush marks. I apply the first coat across the grain, as described above, and let it dry for a minimum of two to four hours. Using P220-grit sandpaper and a block, I lightly

Brush on the Topcoats

Like the primer, the lacquer topcoat is thinned and applied in multiple coats.

BRUSHING RECIPE
60% lacquer, 30% thinner, 10% retarder

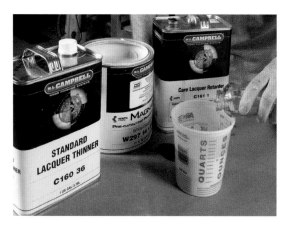

Doctor it for brushing. Thin the topcoat to make it easier to apply and add retarder to leave fewer brush marks.

sand this coat to remove any surface debris and brush marks, and then vacuum away the dust. I apply a second coat of lacquer with the grain, and then allow the workpiece to dry overnight.

Stop here? The next day I assess the workpiece. As long as there is no streaking, and if you like a little grain pattern showing, then you can stop here. If desired, you can rub the surface with 0000 steel wool wrapped around a cork block and then apply

Sand between coats. Sanding not only removes dust nibs and brush marks, but it also creates a mechanical bond between layers of finish.

Brush in sequence. When finishing complicated surfaces, do the large surfaces first with a big brush, then cover molding and trim with a smaller one.

Work horizontally. On large and small pieces, when possible, work on a horizontal surface to reduce the risk of runs.

Choose Your Final Sheen

As with clear coats, you have a choice of final sheen. You can use steel wool and wax for a low-luster look, or pad on the last coat for a high gloss.

PADDING RECIPE
50% lacquer, 40% thinner, 10% retarder

LOW LUSTER

Steel wool and wax. Unwrap a pad of 0000 steel wool and fold it around a sanding block. Rub the surface in one direction to smooth and dull the surface (above). Wipe on and buff off a coat of paste wax (right) for an even sheen and a pleasing feel.

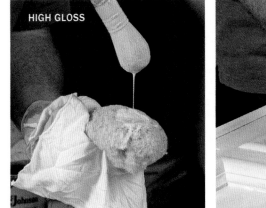

HIGH GLOSS

Pad on a final coat. Make a pad with cotton cloth and cotton wadding. To get an even flow of finish, always add the finish directly to the core (left) and not to the outside of the pad. Pad on a last coat (right), wiping lightly to keep the coat very thin.

Isolate the trim. If you can't pad the whole surface at once cleanly, let the large areas dry overnight, then mask off areas adjacent to the trim and work on it with a smaller pad.

wax, to both level the surface and then even out the sheen.

Brush two more coats and then pad on a topcoat for a flawless finish

Even if you aren't set up to spray, you can still achieve the formal look of a factory finish; it just takes a little longer. Lightly block-sand all the surfaces with P220-grit sandpaper to remove dust nibs and brush marks. Then rub all the surfaces with a maroon abrasive pad, dulling down the finish to make really sure that a mechanical bond can be achieved with the next coat. Follow up by wiping all surfaces with a tack rag to remove any fine sanding debris.

I apply two more coats in the same manner as the first two, sanding after each and allowing for an overnight drying period.

To approach the smoothness achieved by spraying, pad on a final application of lacquer. To form the pad, I cut a cotton bed sheet roughly 8 in. square, removing any hems. I then cut a piece of cotton wadding (available at fabric stores) about 6 in. square and fold it into a wad roughly 2 in. wide and 3 in. long, with a point at one end.

I further thin the topcoat by 10%, and then add it directly to the core of the pad. After squeezing out the excess, I place it in the center of the sheet, bring each corner of the sheet in to the center, twist the corners into a grip for the pad, and make sure that the polishing side of the pad is tight and free of creases or wrinkles.

I start the process perpendicular to the grain, beginning at the far edge, working the pad left to right and slowly moving toward me. When you begin to feel some resistance, it's time to charge the pad with more lacquer. Open the pad and add lacquer to the inner face of the wadding, let it absorb, re-wrap

the pad tightly, and gently squeeze the pad to remove any excess material.

When working in an area where the light source is fluorescent tubes, place the workpiece in a position so that your strokes are perpendicular to the light source for a better surface reading.

Working a small area such as the side of a cabinet, I cover the whole surface two or three times, let it dry for about 10 minutes, and then repeat the process with the grain. I pad in alternating directions up to four times, with a 10-minute drying break after each application, until I am satisfied with the build and evenness of the surface.

In tight corners, moldings, and narrow surface areas, you can try using a smaller pad. Or you can allow the larger surface areas to cure overnight, and then tape them off with low-tack blue tape before padding the adjoining smaller areas.

Let the finish cure for two or three days before moving the piece into the house. This will allow it to off-gas in the workshop and avoid the risk of heavy object imprinting into the finish while it is still soft.

The Hows and Whys of Dyes

Dyes are an indispensable tool for a professional finisher: I use them to give mahogany that rich brown found on antiques, to enhance figured maple, and to brightly color a contemporary piece. However, many woodworkers have a deep fear of coloring wood. I'm reminded of Groucho Marx's witticism: "Die, my dear? Why that's the last thing I'll do!"

In part, this comes from confusion between dyes and pigment stains. Unlike stains, dyes never look muddy or hide the natural beauty of wood. With that in mind, let's take a closer look at what dyes are, where they come from, and how to use them.

What is a dye and how is it made?

For centuries, dyes were obtained from natural products such as roots, berries, insects, and nut husks. Then in the mid-19th century, William Henry Perkin discovered how to make a synthetic purple dye from aniline, an organic compound derived from coal tar. This was a giant step forward: There was now an inexpensive method to mass-produce dyes. Today, most dyes are derived from crude oil but the term aniline is still widely used.

Many woodworkers think that dyes, like stains, are simply finely ground pigments, but this is not true (see p. 154).

The Sum of Its Parts

Dyes are usually a blend of three colors. This can be seen clearly with a water dye. Drop a pinch in water, watch the colors separate, and get a lesson in basic color theory. A reddish-brown dye may contain yellow, orange, and blue. Since orange and blue are complementary colors (opposite each other on the color wheel), they offset each other. In other words, if the dye has more orange than blue, it will be a warmer red brown. Add more blue and the color shifts to a deeper, less reddish brown.

Dyes and Stains Are Two Different Products

A dye is generally an organic compound that is soluble in water, alcohol, or oil. This creates a color in solution that penetrates the wood. Conversely, a pigment remains in suspension and requires a binder to help affix it to the surface. Think of dyes as sugar and pigment as sand. Drop them into warm water and the sugar will dissolve; the sand will collect at the bottom. This is also what makes dyes transparent and stains cloudy.

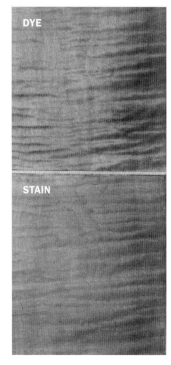

Dyes pop the figure. On close-grained woods like maple, dyes add uniform color while magnifying any figure that is present. Stains muddy the figure.

Stains pop the grain. On open-grained woods, the pigment particles lodge in the pores, highlighting the grain structure. Dyes give a more uniform color.

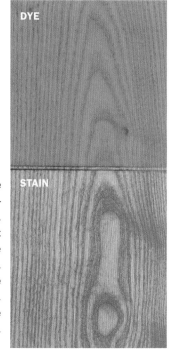

Although you can buy dyes already dissolved, powders offer the widest range of colors and are the most inexpensive option. You also have full control over the color strength by adding powder or diluting the solution.

The three main dye groups associated with woodworking are acid, basic, and solvent dyes. The water-soluble dyes are, for the most part, the acid group, and the alcohol dyes are the basic group. The solvent dyes are soluble in a variety of oil solvents from mineral spirits and naphtha (aliphatics), to xylene and toluene (aromatics), to acetone and lacquer thinners (ketones).

So much for chemistry. Which dye is right for your project?

Water-soluble dyes work for most needs

Water-soluble dyes account for roughly 70% of Lockwood's sales (see the facing page), and there are good reasons for you to focus on them, too. They dissolve easily in warm water, have no odor whether dry or dissolved, and resist fading. They are best applied to new wood and are suitable on any species, but particularly dense-grained species such as maple, cherry, or poplar.

Water-soluble dyes are also easy to apply by hand. On large areas, you want to flood the surface (see the top right photo on the facing page); on smaller areas, folded paper towels or a small brush work well. On very large areas, spraying is an option, and because the dye is water based, there is no need for an explosion-proof spray booth.

The First Family of Colors

Pass it on. Two generations of the Schiffrin family operate W.D. Lockwood, supplying dyes to the woodworking industry.

One of the oldest distributors of dyes in the United States is W.D. Lockwood & Co. in New York City (www.wdlockwood.com). They have been providing their own line of colors to the furniture and instrument-making industry since the late 19th century. They also provide dyes to many companies that repackage them under their own name.

The current owners are the Schiffrin family: Herb, his wife Robin, and their son Jesse. They gave me a fascinating tour of their operation from the filing cabinets full of dye recipes, to the underground vault where the drums of dye powder are stored, and to the mixing facility.

Family secrets. Samples of all the colors Lockwood has made are filed away along with the recipe of how each was formulated.

Each time a color sells out, a new batch must be blended following the secret recipe. To ensure that the new and old colors are identical, white coffee filters are dipped in both solutions and then compared. Simple, yet effective.

Flood the surface. Don't skimp when applying the dye. Plenty of dye yields an even color and you get better penetration if you wet the surface thoroughly.

Uneven application? If you pause on a large surface, you can apply more dye as long as the surface is wet. At first the boundary will be obvious because the earlier dye had longer to penetrate.

Uniform color. After a minute, the boundary will disappear and when the surplus dye is wiped away, the surface will have an even color.

Preparing a dye. Dyes dissolve best in liquid that is around 160°F. If you are heating anything but water, make sure you do it in a hot water bath and not directly over a heat source.

Alcohol dyes dry fast. Alcohol-soluble dyes mixed with some dewaxed shellac are a great way to cover up mistakes such as oversanded edges.

Don't be fooled by the dead look that dyes have when they dry. They come back to life when a clear finish is applied.

The problem of water-soluble dyes raising the grain is overblown. Some boards swell more than others (use a test sample), and for these, dampen the surface prior to final sanding. On all others, any raised-grain fuzziness disappears when you sand the first

coat of clear finish. But what you don't want to do is sand the dye coat, as you will sand through the color in spots.

When preparing your test board, you may find that surface tension prevents these dyes from adding color to the pores of woods like mahogany, oak, and walnut. To ease the surface tension, add a scant drop of dishwashing detergent to the dissolved dye. Don't add too much or you'll get a sudsy dye.

Alcohol-soluble dyes dry fast

The biggest difference between water-soluble dyes and alcohol-soluble ones is that alcohol-soluble dyes dry much faster, generally in less than 15 minutes even when applied by hand. They are considered non-grain raising, which eliminates any need to raise the grain prior to dyeing and makes them excellent for quick touch-ups. Furniture finishers and restorers often have a plastic box with 18 compartments for a wide variety of alcohol-soluble dye powders. Mixing the dyes with a little shellac quickly rectifies finishing flaws such as sanding through color on edges.

On the other hand, while small areas can easily be dyed by hand with a quick-drying solvent like alcohol, it takes careful planning to avoid unsightly streaks when doing a large area. In these cases, spraying is more effective.

Dissolve the powder in denatured alcohol and stir the mixture occasionally for at least an hour. Once the powder is dissolved, you can use the dye to tint finishes such as shellac and lacquer (when tinting lacquer, use a 3:1 mix of methanol and acetone).

All dyes will fade to some degree, but alcohol powders are not as lightfast as water ones. The most fade-resistant dyes are metal-acid complex types. In a sophisticated piece of chemical engineering, a metal such as chromium, copper, or cobalt is liquefied and attached to a molecule of dye in a 1:1 or 1:2

ratio. This creates a much stronger molecular bond and improves lightfastness. TransTints concentrated dye and Solar-Lux NGR dye contain this metal-complex dye, as do some of Lockwood's water-soluble powders.

Oil-soluble dyes are best for tinting

These are probably the dye powders you will use least, but they still have some niche uses. They are useful to add a hint of color in oil-based finishes. By tinting a clear finish, you create a toner that can slightly adjust a wood's color. This is also an easy way to shift a very amber-colored varnish to a more neutral brown. Oil-soluble dyes will dissolve in an aliphatic such as mineral spirits or turpentine but are best dissolved in lacquer thinner, which mixes well with oil-based finishes. Add the dissolved dye in small increments and don't exceed 5% of the finish by volume, or you run the risk of a streaky surface. Less is more here.

Success with dyes

There are a few simple safety precautions for working with dyes. Always wear gloves, and when handling dye powders, wear a dust mask—you only get one pair of lungs.

When mixing a dye, it is best to work by weight vs. volume, but if you lack a sensitive scale, 1 oz. of dye as measured in a plastic medicine dispenser is just under 1 oz. in weight. As you gain experience, you'll get a feel for how much powder is needed to create your colors. The standard concentration is 1 oz. of powder per quart of liquid. However, I normally make a stock solution at twice that strength. If I want to dilute the color, I'll pour some of this stock into a measured amount of clear solvent and test the result. Keep records of the ratios and you can recreate any color.

Dye powders dissolve best in solvents warmed to about 160°F. You can directly heat water (distilled is best), but if you warm up flammable solvent, always use a hot-water

Sneak preview. To see what tinting an oil-based finish will look like, put some finish on a white plate, sprinkle on some dye powder, and rub it around.

Strain the solution. Dissolve the oil-soluble dye in mineral spirits or lacquer thinner, then add it to the clear oil-based finish via a fine paint strainer.

Apply normally. Wipe or brush the tinted oil onto the surface and let it soak in. After waiting a few minutes, wipe up any excess with a clean, lint-free cloth.

Untinted oil

Tinted oil

bath as opposed to open flame or microwave (see the top photo on p. 156). Failure to do so could ruin your day.

Dissolved water-based dyes are susceptible to bacteria, which can form a mold on the surface. However, I keep my dyes in glass or plastic containers out of sunlight and they last a year without problem. Alcohol or oil dyes are not as easily affected by bacteria, but can come out of solution over time and may require stirring and filtering.

If you've never used dyes, you'll be happily surprised at their versatility, brilliance, and clarity. Even though chemists have advanced their quality, some things stay the same. One example is Lockwood's walnut crystals, whose base color comes from a peat found in Germany. Once washed and filtered, it produces a lovely brown we associate with walnut.

Welcome to the wonderful world of dyes.

Why I Don't Use Chemical Dyes

I have deliberately not covered chemical dyes, though a few wood-workers still swear by them. Some, like the vinegar-and-steel-wool concoction, are relatively benign (if you let the hydrogen escape while it brews), but you can get the same color with dye powders with much less hassle. Avoid other chemical dyes at all costs. Potassium dichromate, used to darken cherry and mahogany, contains a heavy metallic salt, hexavalent chromium, which is very dangerous to humans and the environment.

Accentuate Carving with Color

MICHAEL CULLEN

The majority of my carving ends up under several coats of milk paint. This may seem strange to woodworkers used to "bringing out the natural beauty of the wood," but adding color to a carving is one of best ways to highlight the design and to define the pattern.

Because wood grain is a pattern in itself, there is always the potential for it either to compete with the carved pattern or to wholly overwhelm it. What I like best about milk paint is how it combines with the wood to form more of a patina than an opaque coating. It doesn't obliterate the grain; it

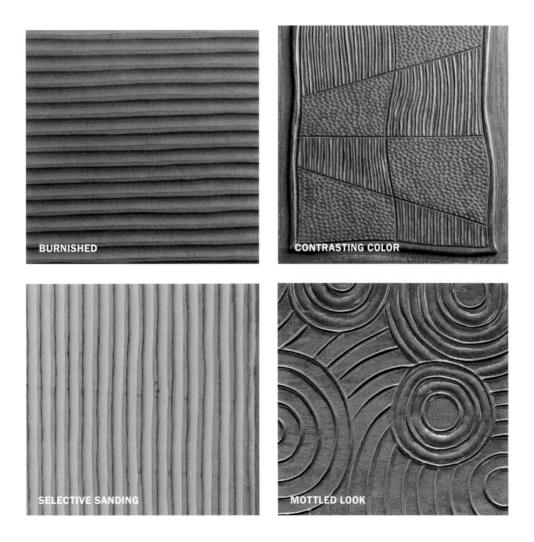

BURNISHED

CONTRASTING COLOR

SELECTIVE SANDING

MOTTLED LOOK

merely tones it down so that the carved pattern can take center stage.

In addition, the paint and my method of burnishing the high points add a sense of depth to the carving, creating subtle highlights in the piece with the changes of hue between the surface and background.

Several coats of one color and a clear topcoat

Make sure the carving is free of dust and that any non-carved surface due to be painted is well-prepped. The paint tends to highlight imperfections, so remove any machine marks. I buy my paint from The Old Fashioned Milk Paint Co. (www.milkpaint.com). The color selection, inspired by colonial New England, is excellent and foolproof. It's virtually impossible to create a bad combination.

Use inexpensive brushes because the lime in the paint is hard on bristles.

Mix Up a Batch

Combine water and paint powder in the ratio recommended on the packet. Let it stand for 10 minutes and then adjust the viscosity to that of heavy cream. The quick-drying paint will stay usable for 24 hours, allowing you to apply multiple coats.

The basic burnished look. Apply coats thinly. Work the first coat into the wood. Aim for a thin, even coating but don't expect to cover all the wood.

Build the paint. Sand the surface only if there are brush filaments or chunks of paint stuck in it. Apply the second coat like the first.

Burnish the high points. After two or three coats of paint, rub the dry surface with 0000 steel wool. This will burnish the paint, smooth the ridges, and reveal some wood on corners.

Clear-coat the paint. A thin coat of shellac is Cullen's favorite for sealing surfaces that will be handled only lightly. Tabletops can receive a more durable finish such as polyurethane.

Wax finishes the finish. To lower the shellac's sheen, apply paste wax with 0000 steel wool and then polish the surface with a soft cloth.

Begin applying the paint in line with the carving, in this case along the grooves of the ripple pattern, making sure the paint is getting down into the grain and that there are no missed spots.

The trick with milk paint is to always maintain a wet edge. If you add wet paint next to dry, the colors will not match, leaving evidence of where you stopped and resumed painting. Touch-ups should be avoided for the same reason—it's safer to repaint the entire surface than to risk highlighting a mistake.

When you've finished the whole piece, let the paint dry for an hour or so. At this point, the painted surface should be dull and chalky to the touch. If there are any nibs or bristles embedded in the paint, remove them with a light sanding with P320-grit sandpaper. Add one or two more coats until the surface is thoroughly covered and appears rich and opaque.

With the color complete, I rub with 0000 steel wool in the direction of the grooves. The objective is to burnish the entire surface and to create an accent of wood peeking through at the carved edges. The burnished paint should appear rich like polished stone and without any cloudiness. As for the exposed wood, lime in the milk paint affects tannins, so mahogany, for example, should appear deep red. If you remove too much paint, leaving too much wood showing through, recoat and repeat the rubbing-out process.

Now apply a clear finish to protect the paint from stains and general dirt. It's important to note that after a clear finish is on, applying more milk paint is no longer an option (milk paint adheres only to itself or to bare wood). If the piece is not going to be handled, then just apply some wax—it's fast and the result is pleasing to the eye. Be aware that the clear coat will deepen and change the hue of the paint.

After the clear coat has dried, use steel wool and paste wax to cut the sheen and give the surface a pleasant feel.

Give one color two shades

This is a great technique because it requires only one color of paint but renders two shades. Apply two to three coats of color to the carving. Next, carefully (and I mean carefully) sand only the flat surface of the carving using P320- or P400-grit no-load sandpaper. Sand lightly to burnish the surface without removing too much paint.

Sand the high spots to create two shades. After the last coat of paint has dried (but before any clear coat), smooth the high points of the surface with P320-grit sandpaper.

Burnish the ridges. Stretch some 0000 steel wool tightly in your hand and move it briskly across the surface, going perpendicular to the grooves. Create a contrast between the darker, burnished ridges and the paler, unaltered milk paint in the grooves.

Contrasting colors. Brush on a couple of thin coats of the base color. Don't aim to get total coverage (top). Once the first color is dry, brush on two coats of a contrasting color (above).

Now, further burnish the surface using 0000 steel wool, making sure to touch the sanded surface only. The top surface should appear polished and the recesses (the carved areas) should appear slightly lighter in hue with a chalky appearance.

You can accentuate the color difference further by applying finish to the burnished areas only. If you get finish in the wrong area, sand it off and apply more milk paint to the carving. This technique should be used only on pieces that will be handled rarely, such as picture frames or candlesticks.

Apply one color over another

Apply two or three coats of the base color as above; then apply a contrasting color until it fully covers the previous one.

Finish the ridges. Apply finish just to the flat surfaces and not in the grooves, using a French polishing-style pad.

Reveal the color underneath. Sand the surface with P320-grit sandpaper and then rub the surface with 0000 steel wool to cut through to the first color in places.

Color and carving combined. When a clear finish is applied, it highlights the two contrasting paint colors as well as the bare wood.

Rub the surface with steel wool until both the first color and the wood show through. The idea is to achieve balance and harmony among all the colors and not have one area appear to be worn more than the rest. When you are happy with the look, add a clear coat and wax.

Apply colors selectively

Apply two or three coats of the base color and don't rub it out. Now dab on streaks of two or more complementary or contrasting colors with a medium-size brush. Blend the colors to give a natural appearance. You can further soften the colors or even remove them by manipulating them with a wet cloth. Sand the surface with P320- or P400-grit paper and/or steel wool until it appears burnished and has the right amount of wood peeking out at the edges. Last, clear-coat and wax the carving.

Dab on color for a mottled look. After the base color is dry, add dashes of complementary colors to the surface. Try to be random rather than deliberate.

Soften the edges. Before the streaks of paint fully dry, dab them with a damp cloth to blend them into each other as well as the base color.

Contrasting carvings. The whole surface was finished in the same way, but the flatter surface of Spring Rain on the right retains more complementary colors, while the ridges on Thousand Suns on the left are sanded through to the wood.

Colorize Your Turnings

JIMMY CLEWES

On many turnings, adding a bright dye can transform a competent piece of work that might not get a second glance into a piece of art that stands out from across the room. Wood turning is a creative craft, and coloring is an even more creative process. Even if you've never applied dye to furniture, I hope you'll break the bonds of inhibition and try dyeing a turning.

When it comes to dyes, my first choices are alcohol-based, and in particular those by Chestnut Products. These are premixed and can be used at full strength or diluted with denatured alcohol. These dyes have a 5% shellac content, so each application progressively seals the wood. Therefore, the later colors soak in less and become more like glazes, creating a layered look rather than mixing into the previous ones.

Two ways to confine the color

Unless you plan to dye the entire piece, you have to create a clean break between the dyed and undyed parts. The safest way is to turn and sand the whole piece, then seal the section that will remain undyed. In this case, I wiped a 1-lb. cut of shellac onto the platter's recessed center, and once that was dry, I applied a coat of Danish oil. If any dye seeps onto the sealed and oiled surface, it comes right off with steel wool. On the other hand, avoid leaving either finish on the section to be dyed or you'll end up with a blotchy appearance.

If you are a confident turner, a quicker method is to turn and sand the area to be dyed, but leave some waste wood on the adjacent section. After the dyes have been applied and dried, come back and turn the rest of the piece, removing the unwanted dye at the same time.

Prep the surface and apply the dye

The surface must be flawless, because any blemishes will show up when you apply the dye. If you are using curly or burl wood (both give pleasing results), the grain may be running in different directions, so inspect the surface very closely.

After the last sanding, raise the grain. I do this by spraying the surface with denatured alcohol because it evaporates quickly. Water works as well but takes longer to dry. Don't resand the wood; you want the dye to penetrate deeply.

Coloring is best done on the lathe: You can turn the piece slowly without touching it by revolving the chuck, and then turn on the power for sanding. Apply the dye with

Alcohol Dyes Are Brighter and Dry Faster

Compared with water-based dyes, alcohol-based ones are brighter and dry faster. You can buy them as liquids or as powders that dissolve in alcohol. Solar-Lux liquids and alcohol-soluble dye powders are available at www.woodworker.com. Chestnut Products can be found online at chestnutproducts.co.uk.

Seal adjacent areas. If you aren't going to dye the whole piece, wipe a washcoat of shellac onto the areas to remain undyed. Follow with Danish oil.

Apply the dye. Start at the inside edge and use the chuck to turn the platter by hand as you dye the wood.

A light sanding. When it's dry, sand the dyed area. You can then move on to the topcoat or add more color.

a brush, cloth, sponge, or folded-up paper towel, but be sure to cover the whole surface evenly and quickly because alcohol-based dyes dry in under a minute. If you do get streaking, quickly wipe the surface with an alcohol-dampened cloth.

Once the surface is dry, lightly sand it with CAMI 600-grit wet-or-dry paper. If you are satisfied with the appearance, you can go

ahead with the clear coat, or apply another coat of the same color.

Layers of color give a dramatic effect

After you've mastered using a single color, there are a couple of ways to use multiple hues. On curly wood, dyes penetrate the short grain more than the long grain. To exploit this effect, let the first color (in this case Chestnut Products' Royal Blue) dry completely, then sand the surface with CAMI 400-grit wet-or-dry paper. This step removes some of the color and leaves a striped effect.

Next, apply a lighter complementary or contrasting color, in this case a more turquoise blue, which will show most where the first blue was removed. Now sand the surface again, this time with CAMI 600-grit paper.

Another Way: Dye First, Turn Later

A more surefire way to get a crisp break between dyed and natural wood is to apply the dye and then complete the turning, cutting away unwanted dyed areas.

Finish the rim. Shape, sand, and dye the rim of the platter, but don't hollow the center.

Finish the center. With the rim colored, use a parting tool to define the inner edge of the rim. Then finish turning the center.

Make the tiger roar. To enhance the stripes of the tiger maple, Clewes sands the first coat with 400-grit paper and then adds more color.

Bolder stripes. On the third round, instead of dyeing the whole rim, Clewes focuses on the darker sections of the curl.

Soften the contrast. If you want the colors to flow slightly together, spray the piece with denatured alcohol. Don't wipe it off.

Easy cleanup. If any dye does get onto the sealed section, 0000 steel wool removes it.

You can either stop here or make the figure pop more with a third color. You can apply the third color to the whole area or just to certain sections. On curly wood, this can be just the lighter parts of the stripes, or on non-curly wood, you can use a dappled pattern. Continue coloring and sanding until you are pleased with the result.

A gloss finish brings the dye to life

While I favor a low- or medium-luster finish for most of my undyed pieces, a thin, high-gloss finish really makes the dyes vibrant and the wood almost iridescent. Although you could wipe or brush on a finish (don't use shellac or you'll pull and blotch the

Quick finish. Gloss lacquer pops the colors, and using an aerosol gets the job done quickly.

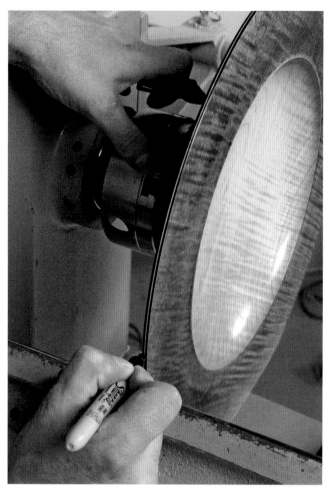

Frame the rim. Coloring the edge of the platter with a permanent marker conceals any dye that bled through and provides a nice break between the dyed and undyed parts of the rim.

alcohol-based dyes), the easiest and fastest finish is spray lacquer. Use a spray gun if you have one, but for small projects like these, an aerosol is economical and won't leave you with a gun to clean.

Spray several light coats of lacquer, letting each coat dry for 20 to 30 minutes. Smooth the surface with CAMI 800-grit wet-or-dry paper followed by 1,000-grit and finally 1,500-grit. For a glasslike finish, buff the piece using liquid car polish.

Texture Wood to Highlight the Grain

GEOFF GUZYNSKI

Light or dark?
Guzynski's texturing method looks great with a clear finish, but if you really want the pattern to pop, try an ebonized treatment (see p. 171).

I've always liked the textured look of weathered cypress. It reminds me of old playground equipment where the wood's texture has been polished by thousands of small hands. It turns out that traditional Japanese craftsmen loved this look, too. They called it jin-di-sugi and created it by burying the wood in the ground and allowing it to decay for several years. I wasn't about to invest that much time, but I was determined to incorporate the look in my furniture. After some experimenting, I came up with a fast and simple technique using an angle grinder fitted with a wire brush.

The process works best on boards with a dramatic difference in density between the earlywood and latewood growth rings. You should be able to run your thumbnail across the grain and leave marks in the earlywood but not in the latewood. I've seen pine, cedar, and fir boards that pass this test, but I've had the best results with cypress. Be sure to test each board individually, however.

The rough and the smooth. The hard, smooth, light-colored beech on Guzynski's credenza complements the soft, dark cypress panels textured to resemble a classic Japanese finish.

Reveal the grain. You need a 4-in.-dia. crimped wire wheel (Milwaukee®, part No. 48–52–5070; www.amazon.com) and a nylon flap brush (Weiler Vortec, model 36447).

Go lightly. Hold the angle grinder so that the wire wheel is parallel to the grain and just touching the surface. The goal is to remove the soft earlywood while leaving the harder latewood intact.

Brush hard. Pull a stiff wire brush across the surface to define the grooves in the earlywood. Use heavy pressure.

Remove the fuzz. A nylon brush attached to a drill removes loose wood fibers and leaves the surface ready for finishing.

Texture the wood in three steps

Dimension the wood in the normal way. It's not necessary to start with a board that's thicker than the intended final thickness because only the softer earlywood is removed. The dense latewood remains unchanged.

Begin removing softwood, keeping the brush's rotation in line with the grain and moving the grinder parallel with the grain. For a less aggressive cut, and to avoid snagging the panel edges, let the brush pull the grinder along the surface.

If you're going to color the wood, the stain mostly penetrates the soft earlywood, so you need to adapt your grinding technique to the grain pattern. In areas where the grain is more flatsawn, use a very light touch with the brush or you will get rid of all or almost all of the earlywood, and the surface won't absorb stain later. A panel with a flatsawn area adjacent to a more quartersawn section would then end up with uneven color. After the grinder, hand-brush the surface with a sparse, stiff-bristled wire brush. The final step is to smooth the panel with a nylon flap brush chucked in a drill.

You can stop here and apply the clear finish of your choice. Be careful to keep any film finish thin because a thick finish that fills the grooves looks really bad.

Dye and stain highlight the texture

Using separate dye and pigment stains allows me to manipulate the color balance between the latewood and earlywood. I start with a very light dye stain in an acetone and water base. The acetone gives the dye a bit more bite on the densest parts of the latewood. I combine brown, red, and yellow dye concentrates from Sherwin-Williams until the mix is a little brighter than if it was the only color being used. If you are using TransTints, Homestead No. 6006 dark mission brown, No. 6010 red mahogany, and sometimes No. 6020 lemon yellow give good results, too.

Once the dye has dried, flood the panel with a black pigment stain, like Minwax ebony diluted with five parts of mineral spirits. Wipe off the excess stain almost immediately. The deep grooves really hold onto the pigment.

Since I spray-finish my work, I don't topcoat the panel before assembling it into the frame. If you are applying finish with a brush, I would definitely recommend a seal coat of shellac before brushing on a topcoat because there is a lot of color you could pick up and drag to the frame.

Kick up the contrast with color. First, dye the surface. Guzynski applies a dye with a slightly brighter color than the intended final look.

Then add a pigment stain. A diluted black pigment stain mutes the dye and also darkens the denser latewood.

A thin coat, please. The textured surface looks best under a minimal clear finish.

Master the Craft of Crackle Paint

NANCY HILLER

If you're looking for a painted finish that's different from the norm, consider crackled milk paint. Though it's most often used in Shaker- or Colonial-style furniture, antique reproductions, and restoration work, you can add crackle finish to almost any piece to create an eye-popping effect. And it has an added bonus: It's nontoxic.

Producing a crackle finish is surprisingly simple. It's brushed on in three steps: a base coat of milk paint, a layer of crackle medium—essentially, thinned hide glue—and last, the topcoat of milk paint. Then get ready to watch the show. As the top layer of milk paint dries, the hide glue layer underneath, with its glasslike surface

Three Coats to Unleash Crackle

1. Undercoat. The first is the undercoat. Brush a coat of milk paint onto bare wood.

2. Glue coat. When the undercoat has dried, brush on a layer of hide glue, the crackle medium.

3. Topcoat. When the glue coat is dry, apply a topcoat of milk paint. Because it doesn't adhere completely to the slick surface of the glue, the paint dries in a crackle pattern.

providing little purchase for the paint, causes it to break apart and form the crackle pattern. Depending on the type and strength of crackle medium you use, you can achieve anything from a fine, filigreed crackle pattern to a much coarser and bolder one. By choosing contrasting colors for the two layers of milk paint, you can emphasize the crackle effect.

Once the topcoat is dry, you can either use your piece as is or seal it with a clear coat to protect the finish from staining by water, oil, and dirt. To arrive at a satisfying crackled finish, it's critical that you experiment and make color samples using the entire process before applying it to a piece of furniture.

Prep the wood and brush on the base coat

Milk paint adheres best to raw wood. Sand the wood to the fineness you desire, and remove dust thoroughly after sanding. Mix the milk paint in a non-metallic container

Bold or fine. Use contrasting colors of milk paint for the undercoat and topcoat to emphasize the crackle. Hiller applies the glue coat full strength for a coarse crackle pattern, and thins the glue for a fine crackle.

First, create the undercoat.
Mix fresh milk paint from powder at the start of each job. Hiller used Federal Blue for the base coat of her cabinet and Buttermilk for the topcoat. Several coats may be required to achieve the depth of color you desire.

Now go with the glue. The crackle medium—either standard liquid hide glue or a proprietary product like Antique Crackle from the Old-Fashioned Milk Paint Co., can be used full strength for a coarse crackle or thinned with water for a finer crackle.

The glue goes on thick. Use a wide brush for quick coverage and straight strokes for a rectilinear crackle pattern. Stippling will produce a more random crackle pattern.

following the proportions recommended by the manufacturer. Apply the base color with a natural-bristle brush or a foam brush. You may need two to three base coats to ensure adequate coverage, depending on the color you are using and the porosity of the wood.

Next comes the hide glue

When the base coat is completely dry, brush on a layer of crackle medium. Franklin Titebond® cold hide glue works well, as do the Old-Fashioned Milk Paint Co.'s Antique Crackle and the Real Milk Paint Company's Natural Crackle.

One shot at good crackle. Apply the topcoat in long strokes with a good-quality brush, well loaded to avoid having to go back.

Best brush for the job. Using brushes sized to the part you are painting makes it easier to cover the area quickly and apply just the paint you need.

Thin the crackle medium with water to produce a finer pattern, or leave it at full viscosity for a bigger, bolder pattern with wider cracks, revealing more of the base color. Thinning by 1:3—one part warm water to three parts liquid hide glue—and applying a thin, brushed-out layer should result in a fine crackle pattern.

You can adjust the pattern not only by changing the viscosity of the crackle medium but also by controlling the thickness of the film and the pattern in which you apply it. Brushing the crackle medium in straight lines, especially at full strength, will typically create a more linear crackle pattern. Stippling with a brush will produce a pattern with fewer rectilinear cracks.

The amount of crackle medium required will vary depending on how thickly you apply it. Expect to use approximately the same volume of crackle medium as you used milk paint for your first base coat. You may use a foam brush or a bristle brush. It's important not to brush out the glue too much, as it can reduce the effectiveness of the crackle.

Allow the crackle medium to dry completely. This will take at least two hours. You can leave it overnight, or even a week or more, without reducing its effectiveness.

Brush on the topcoat

You only get one shot to apply the top color of milk paint, so practice on test pieces. The powder-to-water mixture for this coat of milk paint should be at least 50% powder. Less than that results in foaminess, inadequate coverage, and less crackle. Brush on the milk paint quickly and rather thickly, in straight strokes; if you applied the crackle medium in one direction, brush on the topcoat perpendicular to those strokes to facilitate coverage. You will see the crackle pattern beginning to develop within a few minutes. Once it forms, do not brush over it, as doing so will pull the topcoat off the surface, leaving you with a patch of bare crackle medium ending in a big blob of topcoat.

Clear coat keeps it safe

Allow the topcoat to dry for at least 24 hours. If you plan to apply a protective coating, use a solvent-based finish such as oil-based polyurethane or Danish oil. Don't use water-based protective coatings over a crackle finish—the water will reactivate the crackle medium and leave cracks in the clear coat. Unlike with a regular milk-paint finish, you shouldn't scuff-sand a crackle finish before you apply the protective clear coat; sanding will completely change the look of the crackle, producing a mottled effect. To ensure you end up with the look you want, be sure to include the clear protective coat in your test samples.

Finally, bear in mind that a crackle finish will be hard to dust with a rag, since the texture will catch in fabric. Instead, to keep a crackle-finished piece clean, use a feather duster or a vacuum cleaner with a brush attachment.

For Bigger Crackle, Don't Thin the Glue

Hiller applied cold liquid hide glue full strength to achieve the coarse crackle pattern she wanted for the back boards inside her cabinet. The undercoat color she chose is Mustard, and the topcoat color is Sea Green, both from the Old-Fashioned Milk Paint Co.

Get Started Spraying

TERI MASASCHI

As a professional finisher, I enjoy my work. But let's be honest. Not all woodworkers embrace finishing. That's because the job of brushing or wiping on a finish is time consuming and labor intensive. A faster path to a great-looking finish is to spray it. But the high price of equipment once limited the use of sprayers to commercial shops. Not anymore.

Recently, manufacturers have been rolling out quality high-volume, low-pressure (HVLP) systems with a price that puts spraying within budget for many home shops (see my review of these systems, "Spray for Less," pp. 187–193). These turbine-powered systems do a superb job. Most come in a kit with everything you need to get going and don't require much setup.

The biggest learning curve is mastering the gun—but don't worry. I'll tell you everything you need to know to get great results. We'll start with the gun's controls and how to adjust them, then move on to proper spraying technique. With practice, you'll soon be able to get a professional-quality finish, and get it done fast. Once you've mastered your sprayer, you may enjoy finishing as much as I do.

What to spray and where

For a home shop in the garage or basement, water-based finishes are the only safe option to spray. Solvent-based finishes like lacquer and shellac are highly combustible and require a spray booth equipped with an explosion-proof fan. Water-based finishes aren't nontoxic, just nonflammable, so wear a respirator mask and eye protection while spraying, and wear gloves when pouring finish and cleaning the gun.

You don't need a large space for spraying, but it should be clean, well lit, and have a way of removing the overspray. You can create a simple exhaust system by placing a normal box fan in a window or door to blow air out, with a furnace filter on it to catch the overspray. This will replenish your shop with fresh air and keep those overspray particles from landing on everything in the shop, including your freshly sprayed surface. For instructions on constructing your own spray booth, check out "Make a Simple Spray Booth" by Jeff Jewitt (www.FineWoodworking.com/extras).

Learn the controls

If you've just pulled your new sprayer out of the box and are a little intimidated by all the shiny knobs, don't worry. It's not as complicated as it seems. There are three main controls on the spray gun: fluid volume, fan width, and fan orientation.

Use the fan-width control to match the fan to the work, and adjust it in tandem with the fluid volume—the wider the fan, the more fluid you'll need. You can change the spray pattern's orientation, too. For tabletops or wide upright parts, use a vertical pattern, and for tall surfaces such as bookcase sides,

(Continued on p. 183)

Get to Know the Gun

High-quality HVLP systems are compact and more affordable than ever. It takes a little practice getting familiar with the controls, but soon you'll be spraying furniture like a pro.

Fluid volume. This little knob controls how much fluid you spray. Located behind the trigger, it also serves as the needle's retaining cap.

Power source. The turbine serves as the spray gun's motor, delivering clean, dry air to the gun.

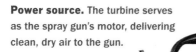

Needles and tips. The needle and fluid tip control the fluid. You have to match them and the air cap to the finish. The gun should come with a set for spraying lacquer-type finishes, and most manufacturers offer more sizes, allowing you to spray a variety of products.

Fan width. Twist the fan-width knob to customize the spray pattern to the job—wide for broad, flat surfaces and narrow for thin parts.

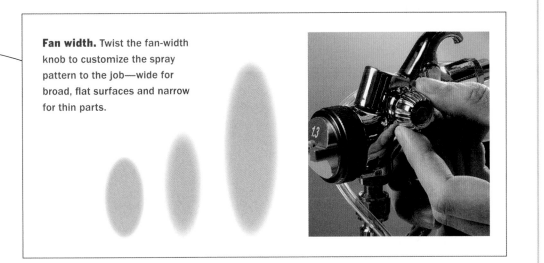

Fan orientation. Switch between vertical and horizontal by rotating the air cap 90°. A threaded ring locks and unlocks the cap.

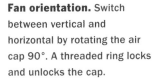

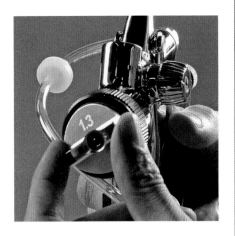

Viscosity cup. You must determine the viscosity of the finish before setting up the gun. Dip the viscosity cup into the finish and time how long it takes for the finish to run through. Stop timing when the stream breaks into drips. Then use a viscosity chart to choose the right air cap, needle, and tip.

Practice with the gun. Before spraying a real finish, get to know the gun and its controls. A low-risk way to do that is with a practice run using dyed water on cardboard. A few drops of dye in the water is all it takes. Pour it into the gun's cup through a paper filter, available from finish suppliers. Filtering your materials will keep the gun free of debris and spraying nicely.

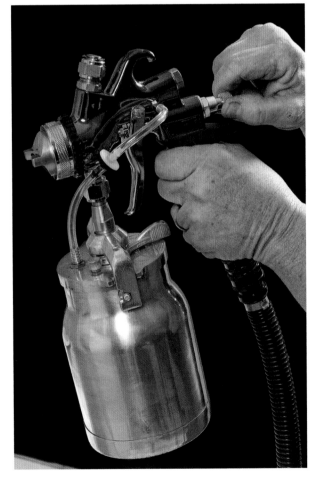

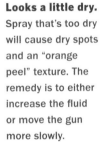

Looks a little dry. Spray that's too dry will cause dry spots and an "orange peel" texture. The remedy is to either increase the fluid or move the gun more slowly.

Too wet. If you're seeing drips, turn down the fluid or move the gun faster.

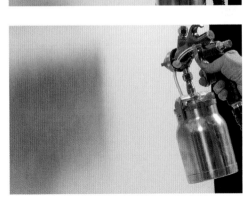

Just right. When you see uniform, wet coverage on the cardboard, with no dry spots or drips, you're on the right track.

Start spraying. Turn the fluid knob to a low setting and gradually dial up the fluid until you get an even finish that's smooth and flat.

Practice Your Technique

Consistently using the right technique can have a big impact on finish quality, so a little effort here to build good habits and muscle memory will improve your finish in the long run.

Start   Finish

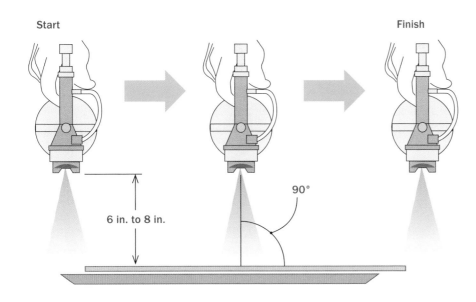

6 in. to 8 in.

90°

Start your stroke early. For the smoothest finish possible, Masaschi pulls the trigger to start spraying several inches before the gun reaches the workpiece.

Consistency is key. Keep the gun at a right angle and 6 in. to 8 in. from the workpiece, and move it at a constant speed.

Don't forget the follow-through. Just like the beginning of the stroke, keep spraying several inches beyond the edge of the piece.

Cross-Hatch Pattern Ensures Uniformity

To keep stroke lines from each pass of the gun from showing up on broad surfaces, coat the surface with light, even strokes with the grain, then while the finish is still wet, turn 90° and coat the entire surface again, working across the grain.

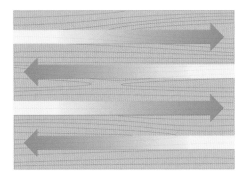

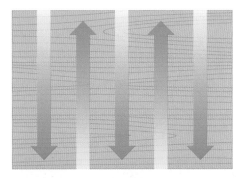

Spraying tops. You'll have to learn to spray horizontal and vertical surfaces, plus wide and narrow areas. A tabletop and base are perfect for teaching the technique. Remove the top from the base and spray them separately so that the overspray from one doesn't get on the other. Spray the bottom of the tabletop first. Coat the underside of the tabletop, using a cross-hatch pattern (left) for even coverage. Use a wide spray pattern and overlap each stroke halfway over the last.

Once dry, flip it over and do the edges. Masaschi dials in a narrow fan pattern for the edges to save material and limit overspray—rogue, partially dried spray particles that can land on other parts of the top, leaving a rough surface on the finish.

Now spray the top. Because the top is the most visible part of the table, Masaschi does it last to eliminate the chance of getting overspray on it. A smooth finish is most important here, so use the cross-hatch pattern again. Let the top dry before doing the next coat.

a horizontal pattern is best. Some systems have an air valve in line on the hose to limit the air pressure to the gun. But limiting the air causes excess wear on most turbines, and most jobs require full-strength air pressure, so it's best to keep the valve open.

Practice makes perfect

Spraying is a learned skill, so get used to the gun and its controls before jumping into a project. You can practice by spraying dyed water on cardboard, placed upright.

Load the gun with the water and connect the air hose to the gun. With the fluid turned off, set the gun to the smallest fan width. Press the trigger and slowly dial up the fluid knob until you get a wet, even spray on the cardboard without drips. Now increase the spray-pattern width to 4 in. or 5 in. wide and dial up the fluid, too, keeping the two adjustments balanced to produce a fine, wet mist. The fan pattern shape should look like a straight line or an oval that's a little fatter in the middle. Next, play with the settings to get more familiar with the gun—change the fan width, and try spraying vertical and horizontal strokes, too.

Once you have a handle on how the gun works, focus on using the right technique. In terms of finish quality, technique is just as important as properly setting up the gun's controls. Hold the gun at a right angle to the surface you're spraying and about 6 in. to 8 in. away: too close and you risk forming drips on the surface, too far and the finish will be too dry and cause a rough "orange peel" texture. The finish wetness is also a function of the rate you move the gun—faster makes it drier, and slower makes it thicker and wetter. Work at a speed that's comfortable for you and keep it consistent as you're spraying, then use the fluid knob to dial in the wetness. To get seamless beginnings and ends to your strokes, start and stop spraying several inches

beyond the edges of the workpiece. To blend stroke lines together so they don't show up in the finish, overlap each stroke halfway over the previous.

Next, try the gun with a water-based coating on some scraps of wood. You'll need to readjust the gun a little when you start— the settings for the finish will be different.

Spraying furniture

Now I'll walk you through spraying a piece of furniture, using the parts of a Shaker table—the broad horizontal top and vertical legs and aprons—as examples. When spraying a tabletop, remove it from the base if possible to avoid getting overspray on the base. Lay it flat at waist height with the top side down, resting on a nail board or painter's pyramids.

Start with a coat of water-based universal sanding sealer (I use a product from Target Coatings). The sealer coat is important; it fills and seals the wood grain, preventing the

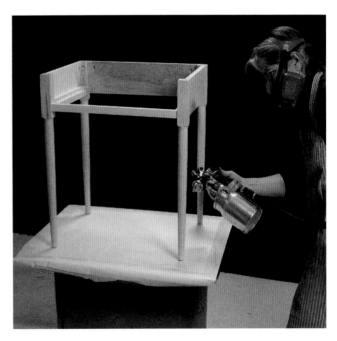

Narrow parts. Work one side at a time. Spray the inner surfaces of the legs, using a medium-width spray pattern a little wider than the legs.

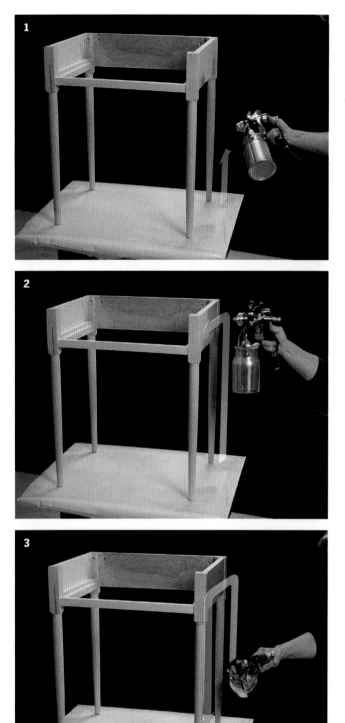

Spray the outer face in one pass. Masaschi starts at the bottom of a leg, goes up and across the apron, then down the other leg with a continuous, smooth motion. Then she returns to the apron to spray any remaining dry spots.

later coats from soaking into the wood and leaving it dry looking, letting you build up a finish with an even sheen in fewer coats. Spray the faces with a wide fan using a cross-hatch pattern (see the drawings on p. 182)—first with overlapping strokes across the grain, then with the grain—to create a more uniform finish. After it has dried for 45 minutes, flip the top over and use a narrow fan to spray the edges, then widen the fan and spray the top.

Let the sealer coat dry, then scuff-sand it by hand with P320-grit paper. Scuffing should produce fine, dry powder. If clumps of finish stick to the sandpaper, let the finish dry longer. Remove the sanding dust by wiping it down with a damp cloth, then spray on two coats of a water-based clear topcoat (I use water-based acrylic lacquer from Target Coatings), scuff-sanding between each coat. If the last coat doesn't come out smooth or has dry spots, let it dry, scuff it and wipe off the dust again, and spray one last coat across the whole surface.

The table base gets the same number of coats, one sealer and two or three clear topcoats. For the legs and aprons on this small table, I used a vertical fan; on a larger job with vertical parts like a tall bookcase, it's easier to use a horizontal fan and move the gun up and down. To avoid drips on the legs, dial back the fluid a little. Spray the base one side at a time, first spraying the inner surfaces, then the outer face. Start spraying at the bottom and move up the leg, turn and spray across the apron, then down the other leg in one continuous motion. After spraying all four sides, let the finish dry and hand-scuff any bumps or drips smooth with P320-grit paper or very-fine grit non-woven abrasive pad between each coat.

Casework. Getting a good finish inside a cabinet isn't always easy, but planning ahead and following a few simple guidelines can really simplify the job. For tall surfaces, use a horizontal fan. Rotate the air cap to spray tall pieces like this bookcase. Make long, overlapping up-and-down strokes to cover the sides.

Remove obstructions. Taking the shelves out of the cabinet before you spray the interior gives you more space to maneuver the gun inside the cabinet, making the whole job easier.

Spray the shelves flat. Laying the shelves and other loose parts flat for finishing is much easier, and you'll end up with a better-quality finish.

Secret weapon. If you give it your best and still get overspray, let it dry, then rub it away with brown kraft paper. If that's not enough, try 0000 steel wool and wool-lube solution.

Load the gun with cleaner. Use a solution of 1 part ammonia and 2 parts water to clean the gun after spraying water-based finish.

Give it a rinse. Hook up the hose and turn on the turbine for a moment to pressurize the gun, then turn it off and spray cleaner through the gun to rinse it out.

Break it down and wash each part. Remove the air cap, fluid knob and needle, and fluid tip and wash them in the ammonia solution. Wash the gun body, too. Wearing nitrile gloves protects your hands from harsh solvents and keeps them clean.

Reassemble and grease the moving parts. Put the gun back together and apply a little petroleum jelly to the needle just in front of the trigger and to the threads of the air cap.

Keep It Clean

Cleaning your gun properly after each use is the best thing you can do to ensure stress-free spraying and will make your sprayer last a very long time. To clean the gun, use a solution of 1 part ammonia and 2 parts water, a clean cotton rag, and a small nylon-bristle brush. Load the gun with the cleaning solution and spray it through the gun. Next, take apart the gun, remove the cup, then the air cap, needle, and fluid nozzle, and place them in a small container of the cleaning solution. Wash the cup and gun body by swabbing them with the ammonia cleaning solution, but never submerge the gun body in cleaner. For stubborn dried-on finish, swab the gun with lacquer thinner. Once clean, wipe them dry with a clean cloth. Scrub the air cap, needle, and fluid tip, then reassemble the gun and lubricate the needle, air cap threads, and the cup rim with petroleum jelly.

To remove any water and finish residue from the gun, load it with a small amount of lacquer thinner and spray it through the gun for 1 or 2 seconds. Leave the thinner in the cup if you'll be spraying again in the next few days. If it's going to be longer than that, empty the cup, dry it out, and put it away—it will be clean and ready to use next time.

The turbine's intake filter can get clogged with dust and cause overheating, so clean or replace dirty filters. Keep the turbine upwind from the gun and off the floor while it's running—it will pick up less dust that way.

Lacquer thinner removes the residue. Load a little lacquer thinner into the gun, pressurize it like before, and spray it through the gun. If you'll be using the gun again within a few days, you can store it with the thinner inside. If not, empty the cup and wipe it dry with a clean cloth before putting it away.

Spray for Less

TERI MASASCHI

If you've considered setting up a spray system for your shop, turbine-powered HVLP systems are the way to go. They take up almost no floor space when you're not using them, and they virtually eliminate setup compared with compressor-driven systems, providing great results right out of the box.

With a low threshold to getting started, you'll get great professional results in a lot less time, letting you breeze through finishing and move on to the next woodworking project quickly. And if you've always shied away from spray systems because of the high prices, there are some new, affordable systems that will make you reconsider.

In this tool test, I looked at 10 different HVLP spray systems available in the United States, with stationary turbines that connect to the spray gun with a hose. I required that the sprayers be compatible with both water- and solvent-based lacquer, and I tested them using both. Most important, I wanted to see if these spray systems deliver a professional-quality finish.

The guns divide into two different styles. Those that continue to spray air when the trigger is released are called "bleeders," while guns that stop spraying air when you release the trigger are called "non-bleeders." Non-bleeders are nicer to use because you don't have to worry about where the gun is pointed when you're not spraying, and you

The Top Performers

If you're looking to create professional-quality finishes quickly, these three sprayers won't let you down. They all excelled in finish quality and comfort and were the most intuitive to adjust.

Fuji Spray Mini-Mite 3™

The Fuji had a wider spray pattern than the others, and the pattern maintained a consistent shape, which was impressive. The non-bleeder-style gun has a very comfortable grip and features an easy-to-reach fan-width adjustment knob on the side. As the lowest-priced option of the Best Overall winners, this system also gets a Best Value award.

Apollo Eco-3/E7000 gun

This system is a great performer, producing a fine mist with a nicely shaped spray pattern that's convenient to adjust using a knob on the back of the non-bleeder-style gun. The cone-shaped interior design of the cup is a unique feature that keeps the gun from spitting air when it gets low on material, a plus.

Earlex® SprayStation HV 5500

Despite its low price, this gun does not compromise on comfort or spray quality. The cup has a protective coating inside to prevent corrosion, and the air cap adjusts with nice action. The air hose connects to the top of the bleeder-style gun, which cramps finger space for the fluid knob below, but the solid performance makes the gun an amazing value.

avoid the risk of blowing dust into a freshly sprayed finish. As I used the sprayers, I also evaluated them on the adjustability of the gun controls, ease of loading and cleaning, and how comfortable each gun handle was to hold while spraying.

The proof is in the pattern

The first thing that really separated the guns from one another was the spray test. To achieve a smooth, even finish, a spray gun must produce a fine mist with a symmetrical or slightly tapered fan-shaped pattern in a nice straight line. To test each sprayer's ability to break finish into a really fine mist, I sprayed black-tinted water-based lacquer and black solvent-based lacquer onto white cardboard. The dark finish allowed me to clearly see the shape of each gun's spray pattern, as well as how fine a mist each gun was able to create. Water-based lacquer is much safer and more widely used these days, but it's more difficult to split up into a very fine mist, so it was a challenging test for the sprayers.

The Fuji Spray Mini-Mite 3, Apollo ECO-3, 3M, Lex-Aire, Earlex SprayStation HV 5500, and Earlex SprayPort HV 6003, systems all did well in this round of tests.

Comfort is critical

When you're holding onto something for an hour or more at a time, comfort can be a very big deal. There are many good designs among the sprayers tested, so you won't have to compromise on this feature. We tested the gun handles for both small and large hands and then averaged the scores, but the scores were pretty consistent between the two. The top scorers on comfort were the Apollo, the Fuji Spray Mini-Mite 3, and the 3M.

Conventional controls. Many guns have separate knobs that adjust the fluid volume and the air volume, which in turn control the width of the spray pattern. This traditional system, as seen on the Earlex SprayPort, is straightforward.

Coating protects. The Earlex SprayStation has a cup with a protective coating inside that guards against corrosion.

Spray adjustments should be simple

To test the adjustability of each sprayer, I focused on ease of adjustment, intuitive design that doesn't leave you guessing at which knob to turn, smooth action, and convenient placement of the knobs that doesn't interfere with other gun features. The SprayPort, the ECO-3 with the E7000 gun, and the Fuji all were simple to adjust, fast and intuitive to figure out, and had overall nice fit and finish, allowing you to turn the knobs with a light twist of the fingers. The controls on these systems also adjusted the spray width from an even, wide pattern down to a small circular one almost effortlessly.

Three sprayers rise to the top

In the end, two systems emerged as Best Overall: the Apollo ECO-3 with the E7000 non-bleeder-style gun, and the Fuji Spray

Spitproof. The cup from the Apollo ECO-3/E7000 system has a cone-shaped bottom, which helps keep the gun from picking up air when the fluid gets low—a helpful feature.

Watch out for threaded cups. The threads, shown here on the Wagner Flexio® 890, are difficult to clean, and once they form a buildup of old finish, they become hard to use.

In the way. The hose on the Earlex SprayStation is close to the fluid-adjustment knob underneath, making it harder to turn the knob and also to spray in tight spaces.

Out of the way. The hose on the Fuji Spray Mini-Mite 3 attaches out of the way at the end of the handle and has an easy-to-grip coupling that makes it a snap to attach.

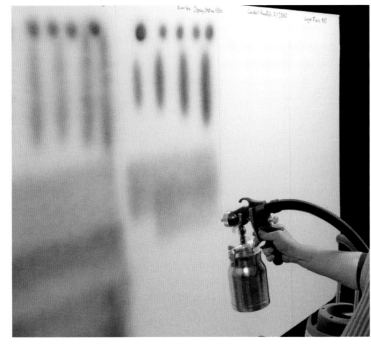

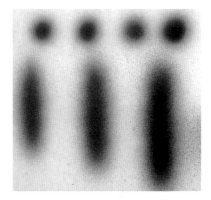

Good pattern. You want a tapered, symmetrical spray pattern that makes it easy to lay down an even coat of finish and overlap strokes without leaving lines behind.

The bottom line: How well do they spray? Masaschi tested each system by spraying dark-colored solvent-based and water-based lacquer onto white cardboard, making it easy to see the size of the spray droplets and the shape of the spray pattern.

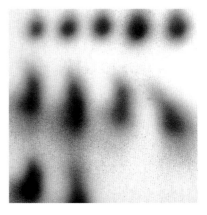

Poor pattern. A sloppy or pear-shaped spray pattern makes it almost impossible to blend overlapping strokes together.

The Bottom Line: How Well Do They Spray?

Model	Ease of Adjustment	Spray Quality	Comments
(BEST OVERALL) APOLLO ECO-3/ E7000 GUN	Excellent	Excellent	Non-bleeder-style gun is comfortable to use and simple to adjust. System produces a nice spray pattern.
EARLEX SPRAYPORT HV 6003	Excellent	Excellent	Air and fluid knobs located on the back of a non-bleeder-style gun, making it easy to dial in a nice spray pattern. The system had plenty of power, but the gun was not as comfortable as several others.
(BEST VALUE) EARLEX SPRAYSTATION HV 5500	Good	Very good	Great performance with a comfortable bleeder-style gun and simple controls.
(BEST OVERALL)(BEST VALUE) FUJI SPRAY MINI-MITE 3 T-SERIES	Excellent	Excellent	Gun has a comfortable handle and a dedicated spray-width adjustment knob. The spray pattern was consistent and impressive.
GRACO® FINISHPRO 7.0	Good	Good	This gun worked well but sprays fast and heavy, making it better suited to professionals covering large areas. The non-bleeder-style gun has a comfortable handle and the system packs nicely into the carrying-case-style turbine.
LEX-AIRE LX-60C	Fair	Very good	Air volume and spray pattern on this bleeder-style gun are both controlled by adjusting the air cap, which was stiff and difficult to turn.
ROCKLER HVLP SPRAY SYSTEM	Poor	Poor	Cup mounts to gun with threads, making it difficult to clean. The gun handle is uncomfortable, and the bleeder-style gun could not be adjusted to spray a fine mist. Hose attaches to top of the gun and often got in the way.
3M 23K-PRO 1	Very good	Very good	This non-bleeder-style gun worked well and was comfortable to hold. But it uses a cup system with disposable liners that added inconvenient steps to the process.
TITAN® CAPSPRAY™ 75	Poor	Good	This non-bleeder-style gun produced a nice spray pattern but sprays fast and heavy, making it better suited to professionals covering large areas. Gun was not very comfortable, with overly complicated adjustments.
WAGNER FLEXIO 890	Poor	Poor	Convenient on/off switch on the body. Produced a nice spray pattern, but not a very fine spray. There is no hook to hang the spray gun from, and the hose is permanently connected to the gun, so it tips over easily.

Earlex SprayPort HV 6003

Graco FinishPro 7.0

Lex-Aire LX-60C

Rockler HVLP Spray System

3M 23K-Pro1

Titan Capspray 75

Wagner Flexio 890

Mini-Mite 3. Both had superior quality spray, very comfortable handles, and easy-to-use, ergonomic adjustment knobs that adjust the spray very nicely.

For the Best Value award, the Fuji Spray Mini-Mite 3 and the Earlex SprayStation HV 5500 both win. If you want to start spraying but the Fuji is still a little out of reach, the Earlex SprayStation is even more affordable and has a great spray quality, if you don't mind compromising on a few adjustability features.

Switch to Spraying Water-Based Finishes

TERI MASASCHI

The first time I used a water-based finish, I promised it would be my last. In the late 1980s and 1990s, companies launched a mass of water-based finishes and used the consumer as the testing lab. I wasn't alone in finding the new finishes too difficult, too finicky, and too unpredictable.

Twenty-five years later, the air-quality laws are more stringent than ever and the end is approaching fast for many solvent-based finishes. The good news is that during this period, the formulators of water-based finishes have been busy. As a hardened "lacquer head," I never thought you'd hear me say this, but when it comes to water-based finishes, I like what I have used recently.

Switching to water-based finishes has been a relief: No more headache or solvent hangover at the end of a long day, and far less use of flammable solvents. However, the transition has not been easy, in part because solvent lacquer and water-based lacquer are as alike chemically as chalk and cheese (see "Not Your Dad's Lacquer" on p. 196). Therefore, fellow lacquer heads have to forget much of what they know and in some ways become novice sprayers again. However steep

Choose your gun carefully. Water-based finishes will corrode an aluminum cup. Instead, make sure the cup and the gun's fluid passages are either stainless steel or plastic. 3M's PPS system of plastic cups with disposable liners works well.

Aluminum   Stainless steel   Plastic

Clear the air. Water-based finishes are very sensitive to contamination. Use a filter to remove moisture and oil coming from the compressor.

No tack cloth, please. Use a damp cotton or microfiber cloth to wipe away sanding dust. A sticky tack cloth can leave residue that will repel water-based finishes.

the learning curve, it is well worth the climb. And for newcomers to spraying, here is your chance to finally achieve professional-looking finishes without the need for an explosion-proof spray booth.

The right tools and conditions are critical

One thing that hasn't changed is that water-based finishes remain generally fussier than solvent-based ones. Your spray gun needs to have either stainless-steel or plastic fluid passages because water-based finishes corrode aluminum quickly.

Everything must be clean, clean, clean! Keep the surface contaminant-free, the gun dedicated to water-based finishes, the air source (if compressor driven) filtered to remove moisture and oil, and the spray gun's cup clean (a disposable lining is best).

I have sprayed solvent-based finish as low as 45°F and gotten away with it, but water-

Not Your Dad's Lacquer

For 80 years, nitrocellulose lacquer has been the benchmark against which all other finishes are found wanting. Each coat melts into the previous one, creating a single film of finish no matter how many coats are applied. This creates the dimensional and reflective sheen that allows you to look down into the beauty of the wood.

Trying to associate their new finishes with the industry standard, manufacturers started calling many water-based formulations lacquer. However, the ingredients of the two have nothing in common. Water-based lacquers usually consist of a glycol solvent, an acrylic resin, a glycol ether, and various leveling agents, defoamers, and other performance enhancers. This is not your father's lacquer but it will, most likely, be yours.

To warm up the color, seal first with tinted shellac. If you don't like the cool look of a water-based finish on some darker woods, warm up the wood by applying dewaxed shellac tinted with a dye concentrate (www.homesteadfinishingproducts.com) as a sealer.

Or tint the finish. You can tint the finish with one or more dye concentrates (www.woodworker.com). If you use water-soluble dye powders, mix the dye in some warm water before adding it.

based finishes are more temperature sensitive. The safe range is about 60°F to 80°F.

One thing you don't have to worry about is compatibility with no-load sandpaper, which has stearates to prevent the paper from gumming up. Stearates used to leave a waxy coating that fouled up water-based finishes, but modern stearates don't have this problem.

Anyone who has refinished old furniture is familiar with "fisheye," the shallow craters in the finish caused by contaminants, in particular silicone. You can add a fisheye destroyer to solvent-based finishes but not to water-based ones, so if you are working on antique furniture, be prepared to use shellac as a sealer coat over the contaminants first. On most woods, it isn't necessary to pre-raise the grain before spraying a water-based finish, but you should on gnarly or figured wood.

How to warm up the color

One of the main differences between solvent- and water-based finishes is the latter's cold appearance and inability to warm the wood. If you are finishing maple, birch, ash, or any white wood, water-based can be perfect. On cherry, walnut, mahogany, or figured woods (including maple), it isn't. You can solve the problem by tinting the coating with an amber dye to mimic the tone of solvent lacquers and oil-based products. But water-based finishes have a milky appearance at first, making it hard to judge the tone.

A better approach is to coat the bare wood with dewaxed shellac. You can tint light-colored shellac such as beige or blond, or use darker grades such as orange or garnet. This eliminates any need to pre-raise the grain. Also, if you wipe on a coat of oil to enhance a wood's figure, apply a coat of dewaxed shellac before using a water-based finish.

Big pluses: faster build, fewer fumes

If the preparations for spraying water-based finishes are more elaborate than for their solvent siblings, the actual spraying is easier. Unlike solvent-based lacquers, which tend to be sticky and syrupy, water-based coatings spray thin and wet but have excellent "cling," which means fewer sags and runs. They dry in about the same amount of time as solvent-based ones—30 to 45 minutes. With any type of finish, the number of coats is subjective. However, because the solids content of water-based finishes is generally higher than for solvent-based ones, you will be pleasantly surprised after only the second coat. This faster build offsets the fact that water-based finishes cost 20% to 30% more.

Filter first. Before spraying, pour the finish through a fine-mesh paint filter to remove any contaminants that could block the gun.

No fancy booth needed. If you don't have a purpose-built spray booth like this one, build a simple knock-down one. An exhaust fan draws air through the filters, pulling away overspray.

Sand between coats. With a quick-drying, water-based finish in a clean environment, you shouldn't need to sand away dust nibs between coats. However, if you let the finish dry for longer than the time specified on the can, you must sand the surface to give the next coat a mechanical bond.

Brown bag: a pro's secret weapon. You can use brown shopping-bag paper to smooth and polish the last coat of a satin or semi-gloss water-based finish.

Use a small setup for the gun, such as Accuspray™'s 0.043-in. needle and a No. 5 aircap. You could use a No. 7 aircap for a large surface. After prolonged spraying, crusted coating may build up on your spray gun. I apply a thin film of Vaseline® on the horns of the air cap first, so I can flick off the buildup later with my fingernail.

Water-based finishes are safer—

The moment when solvent finishes are the most dangerous is not when spraying them—you're wearing a respirator and the fan is drawing off the fumes—but when they have just dried. You've removed your respirator and are scuff-sanding the surface. The fan has been shut off, but all the solvents are lifting off the surface and hanging heavy in the air. This is incredibly lethal exposure. Water-based products give off gas, too, but are far less toxic. The gas has a smell similar to mild ammonia.

Rubbing out and cleaning up

Most water-based materials contain a blend of resins such as acrylics and urethanes that offer durability and clarity, and you can often get a perfect finish off the gun, particularly for a satin sheen.

However, if you want a polished-out surface, don't assume that these coatings are going to behave like solvent lacquer. Successive coats do not melt completely into the previous layer. In this way, water-based finishes are more like solvent-based varnishes or polyurethanes in that the finish builds in layers rather than melting into a single film. Consequently, there is a higher risk of "witness lines" when you polish through one coat into another.

The solution is to apply two or three coats and then completely flatten the surface. This will create numerous white witness lines, but they will disappear when the next couple of coats are applied. You can then polish the last coat with less risk of burning through the layers. Cure time for a successful rubout is the same as for solvent-based finishes: A minimum of 200 hours is preferable.

When you are done spraying, flush and clean the gun with water and ammonia, and then flush it with alcohol or lacquer thinner (you can't escape flammable solvents entirely).

Go ahead and use the new generation of water-based finishes. Just don't try them at the last moment! It is much less stressful to use test samples, and get a feel for these products first.

Don't Overlook Aerosols

TERI MASASCHI

Top Five Types, in Order

There is an amazing variety of aerosols on the shelves of home centers and hardware stores. To help narrow your choice, here are five types of finish ranked in order of usefulness.

1. DEWAXED SHELLAC

If you buy only a single aerosol finish, pick this one. You can use it throughout the finishing process from sealing bare wood to isolating individual finishing steps such as dyeing or glazing, and finally as a clear topcoat. As with any dewaxed shellac, it is compatible with all other finishes.

2. NITROCELLULOSE LACQUER

This clear topcoat is more durable than shellac and dries faster. Unlike shellac, it is available in matte, satin, and gloss. There are many brands and it is widely available. The strong odor is a drawback.

3. OIL-BASED POLYURETHANE

It's best used as a topcoat over brushed-on coats of polyurethane, combining a smooth topcoat with thick-film durability. It is available in satin, semigloss, and gloss.

4. SPAR URETHANE

Since aerosol spray can only be applied as a thin coat, the three coats recommended on the can will not provide exterior durability. You'll need to apply eight to 10 coats for resistance to the harsh outdoors of any climate.

5. STAINS AND TONERS

These aerosol colors are great for touchups and repairs where the color can be blended in. Just don't try to get even coverage over a large surface.

Is there anyone who hasn't picked up an aerosol for some reason? Also known as rattle cans or spray bombs, they're used for everything from air freshener to knocking out wasps' nests. Yet when I tell woodworkers that I'm a frequent user of aerosols for finishing wood, most of them assume I'm either a bad finisher or somehow I'm cheating.

When finishing small projects such as boxes and picture frames, the canned convenience of aerosols is irresistible. It simply isn't worth getting a brush dirty or filling a spray gun—the cleanup alone will take more time than the finishing. Also, if you aren't set up to spray, aerosols are a cheap way to get a topcoat with that flawless, off-the-gun finish. And last, aerosols are available for almost every finish: solvent-based nitrocellulose or acrylic lacquers, shellac, oil-based polyurethanes, paint, stains, and toners.

How to get the best from an aerosol

An aerosol can't compete with a spray gun in terms of flexibility, power, or endurance. However, if you select your projects carefully, you can get a flawless finish with an aerosol at a fraction of the cost of a spray gun and in a fraction of the time of a wipe-on finish.

You just need to understand an aerosol's limitations. Whether brushing or spraying, you must apply a strip of finish while the adjacent one is still wet so that the two flow together. But aerosols apply finish fairly slowly; when combined with thin, fast-evaporating finishes, this makes keeping a wet edge almost impossible when you have to do long strokes across a very large surface. If you try, you're very likely to get a striped effect where wet finish was laid down next to finish that had already dried. The top for a night stand is about the limit for fast-drying

Problem. Because aerosols lay down a narrow band of finish, it is more difficult to overlap adjacent strokes, but failure to do so leaves a striped effect on the surface.

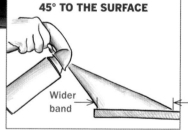

Solution. Holding the can at around 45° to the surface creates a wider spray fan on the workpiece. This helps overlap strokes to achieve an even coating, but you need to move the aerosol more slowly.

finishes such as shellac, solvent lacquer, and water-based finishes. You could probably finish a small coffee table if you use an oil-based polyurethane.

Some finishers recommend spraying across the grain and then immediately with the grain, a method known as cross-hatching, as a way of ensuring even coverage. I've found that unless you are working on a tiny surface, this technique will leave a checkerboard

Get a Handle on It

Using an aerosol for any length of time can leave you with a nasty case of "spray finger," a painful digit locked in a cramped curve. The solution is a can handle, which gives the aerosol more of a spray-gun feel. There are various models on the market for $3 to $5, and any of them will work on most spray cans.

pattern when the finish dries. Instead, spray with the grain but overlap each stroke by 25% to let the wet edges blend together. Use back lighting to help you see this overlap clearly. You want to keep the can's nozzle an even 6 in. to 8 in. from the workpiece. Don't swing the can in an arc by pivoting from your shoulder or wrist; instead, move the can parallel to the workpiece, keeping your wrist stiff. I can't give you an exact speed to spray at because different brands spray different volumes. Instead, go slow enough to just get an even, wet, shiny surface but fast enough to avoid puddles or runs.

Seal small projects with shellac. It is a good idea to seal bare wood with a coat of dewaxed shellac. To avoid having to touch the piece or walk around it, place it on painter's pyramids that rest on a lazy Susan.

Sand the sealer. The first coat almost always causes some raised grain, so lightly scuff-sand it with some P320-grit sandpaper and then remove the dust.

A durable topcoat. For lightly handled objects, three or four coats of solvent lacquer give plenty of protection and the finish can be done in a day. Spray the inside of the box first and the outside last. In this way, any overspray is on the less-visible surfaces.

Don't fear the fretwork. Finishing this pierced corbel with a cloth or an artist's brush would be tedious. But an aerosol gives a flawless finish in no time at all.

Highlight carved surfaces. Using a brush to finish carved surfaces can leave pools of finish in recesses. Aerosols give an even finish.

If you don't have any kind of spray booth, it is a good idea to have a fan adjacent to you set on low to push overspray away from the project. It is also a good idea to cover any surface within about 8 ft. of the workpiece to protect it from overspray.

Top off a table or finish off a box

A good example where selective use of an aerosol can be really helpful is a bedside table. While a low-build, wipe-on finish is fine for most of the piece, the top should have a more durable coating. On this area, brush on three coats of a durable film finish such as lacquer or polyurethane, sand away any brush marks or dust nibs, and then use an aerosol to add three or four flawless coats to the tabletop. If you can't detach the tabletop, mask off the rest of the table. Be sure to use the same product line for brushing and spraying, such as Deft brushing lacquer and then Deft aerosol lacquer, or the two versions of Minwax's oil-based polyurethane.

If an aerosol coat ends up a mess, sand it with P320-grit sandpaper, remove all the dust, and then try again.

For many small projects or components, an aerosol finish is ideal. A small box, for example, doesn't need much finish, so cost isn't a factor, and keeping a wet edge is no problem. Handling such a piece while brushing or wiping a finish is awkward, but with an aerosol you simply place the box on a nail board or painter's pyramids and walk around the piece as you spray. Better still, use a lazy Susan. These fast-drying finishes aren't a magnet for dust and debris, and you can apply two or three coats in a day. Just don't try to apply one fat coat, or all you'll get are drips and runs.

Other handy uses

Another use for aerosols is to seal the surface during a multi-step finishing process. Sprayed shellac seals or "sets" the color without smearing it. Later, if the surface has been glazed, a spray coat of shellac or lacquer seals the color work before topcoating.

To clean up, simply invert the can and squeeze the trigger for a couple of seconds to clear finish from the nozzle. There's no brush or spray gun to clean laboriously and no oily cloths to worry about.

Don't ruin your dye job. Seal in the color. Wiping on a sealer coat of shellac can reactivate and remove some of the dye you are trying to protect.

Perfectly protected. You can spray a sealer coat of shellac over even an alcohol-soluble dye and not cause any blotching.

A Refillable Aerosol

An alternative to aerosols is a system made by Preval®, which gives you roughly four times the spraying capacity as a regular aerosol can for about the same price. Pour any thinned material into the 4-oz. glass jar, screw it to a replaceable power unit, and then start spraying. The power unit can spray at least 16 oz. before it needs to be replaced. The reusable jar can also be capped and the material stored for another time. The spray isn't as fine as a typical aerosol, but it's good for sealer coats. You can also spray a greater range of finishes such as custom-tinted clear finishes or darker grades of shellac.

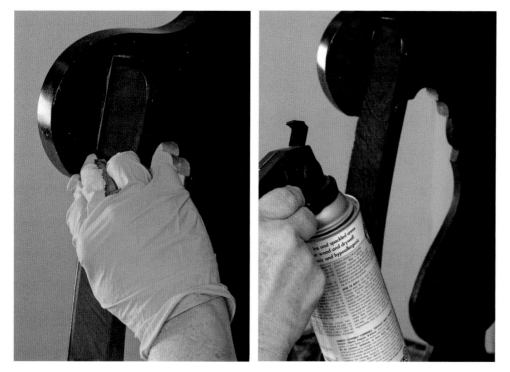

Invisible repairs. Apply the ground color, then seal it in. Wipe on a dye that closely matches the predominant color of the undamaged areas (left). Spray on a coat of shellac to isolate the base color (right).

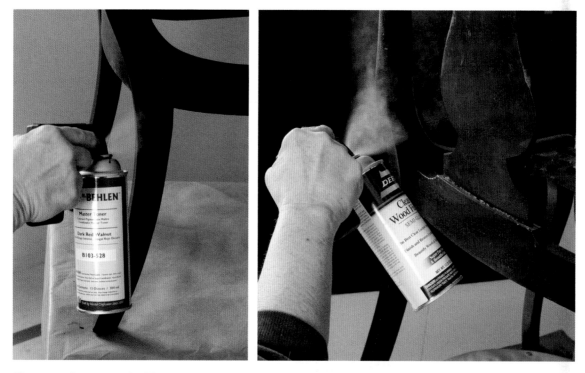

Fine-tune the tone and add a topcoat. Use an aerosol toner to blend the color of the repair into the rest of the piece (left). Spray on a clear topcoat to complete the repair (right). Aerosol clear finishes come in different sheens. Apply the color and the clear coat in light bursts while holding the can farther from the surface to blend in the repair.

Revive
a Finish

JEFF JEWITT

Stripping a piece of furniture must be the nastiest finishing task. Not only are the fumes unpleasant, but it's also messy and requires cumbersome safety equipment. Yet for many, stripping is the first thing that comes to mind when they see a piece of furniture whose finish is worn or damaged. However, stripping is the nuclear option of refinishing.

In many cases, if the finish is just worn but still in good shape, you should consider cleaning and reviving it. This approach is used extensively in the antiques and museum trades and uses simple materials and surprisingly few tools.

I'll show you several no-strip methods for refreshing different kinds of finish. I'll discuss which finishes respond well and which don't. Go ahead and experiment on an old piece. You'll most likely be amazed at the results, but if you aren't, you can always strip it afterward without having invested a great deal of time.

Ready for revival. After 30 years, the original penetrating oil finish on this table is still intact but has become dull and is obscured by a layer of dirt and grime. The fix isn't refinishing, but cleaning and renewing the finish.

Evaluate the Finish

IS IT BEYOND REPAIR?
To see if any finish is worth reviving, wipe it down with some paint thinner or mineral spirits. Wetting the surface not only helps you preview what the piece will look like under a revived finish, but, more importantly, it also reveals any major flaws in either the finish or the wood that can be fixed only by stripping the piece.

Missing finish
You can't revive a finish if it's missing. The mineral spirits will darken areas with no finish.

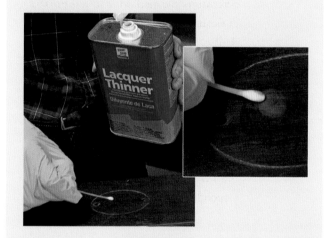

WHICH TYPE ARE YOU DEALING WITH?
Oil finishes are easy to spot, but a film finish could be a number of things. Rub a cotton swab soaked in lacquer thinner on an unobtrusive area. If the finish comes away, it is lacquer. If it doesn't, try denatured alcohol to see if it is shellac.

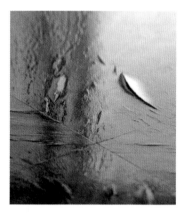

Damage to the wood
Cracks and blisters in veneer make reviving a finish pointless. On solid wood, if long, deep scratches and gouges have gone through the finish into the wood, cleaning and reviving may make them look worse.

Black/gray areas
Cleaning and reviving will not remove gray or black areas. These problems usually indicate water damage to the wood and not the finish.

Sticky finishes
Finishes around pulls that are routinely in contact with skin will become sticky over time. If you press a cotton swab on the finish and parts of the cotton remain, go right to stripping. Cleaning and even putting new finish over a sticky finish will never harden it.

Alligator skin
Some finishes that have been applied thickly become brittle and crack as they get older. The resulting finish is rough and bumpy. Don't bother trying to clean or revive these finishes.

Evaluate the damage and determine the finish

Woodworkers usually get to finish new furniture, but there are a couple of reasons why it is good to know how to refinish a piece. The finish on your early creations may have deteriorated, or perhaps you own an heirloom or two or couldn't resist a flea-market bargain. The first step is to see if the finish has damage that puts it beyond reviving (see the photos on the facing page).

If it looks like a good candidate for reviving, the second step is to see what type of finish you're dealing with because this determines the method. The best finishes to clean and revive are old oil, oil/varnish, shellac, and lacquer finishes. The first two types are generally wipe-on, penetrating finishes with little to no surface build and will have a flat, dull look when old. You may even have applied them yourself when you built the piece.

With a film finish, test to see if it is lacquer or shellac (see the facing page). If the finish responds to neither solvent, it is probably oil-based polyurethane, a waterborne finish, or a high-tech catalyzed finish, none of which revive very well. However, you can still put these finishes through the two-step cleaning process explained below.

A good cleaning reveals the finish

First, remove any loose dust from the surface. Next, take a rag, ideally with a little texture such as terrycloth, and wet it with mineral spirits or paint thinner. Rub the surface in small circles, paying attention to crevices and corners that might contain old wax as well as areas that get contact with hands and fingers, such as around knobs and pulls. I often wear a respirator when using either solvent indoors, but if you work in a well-ventilated area (as I am below) you can probably get by without one. Or you can substitute odorless mineral spirits (Klean-Strip is one brand) or naphtha, which evaporates faster and doesn't have a lingering solvent odor.

If you don't see a lot of grime on your rag when you do this step, all that means is that

A TWO-STEP CLEANING PROCESS.
To start, remove the wax and grease. Dampen a cloth with paint thinner, and rub the surface. This will take off any residual wax polish.

Now clean the surface. Warm water and dish detergent remove the accumulation of dirt from sticky fingers, spilled food and drink, and any leftover paint thinner.

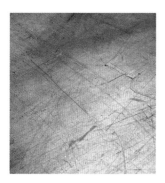

RESTORE AN OIL FINISH.

Thin, wipe-on finishes don't offer much protection, so over the years the surface becomes scratched. Fortunately, they are easy to revive.

Wet-sand and wipe. Pour on a liberal amount of a wiping varnish and then sand the surface with fine sandpaper (inset). This removes most of the scratches and leaves an even sheen. Once you've sanded the whole surface, wipe off the extra finish and let the piece dry (above).

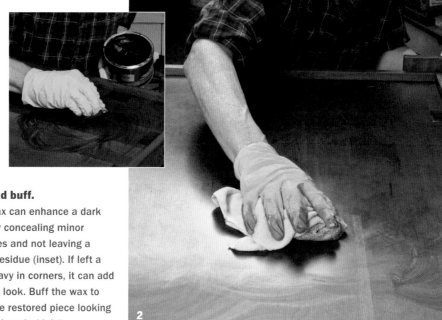

Wax and buff.
Dark wax can enhance a dark wood by concealing minor scratches and not leaving a cloudy residue (inset). If left a little heavy in corners, it can add an aged look. Buff the wax to leave the restored piece looking beautiful again (right).

the finish probably wasn't waxed often or exposed to oil-based products such as lemon oil. However, if there's some grime on the surface that doesn't seem to be coming off with the cloth, you can use a piece of 0000 steel wool.

For the second cleaning, put about ½ oz. of dish detergent in a pint of lukewarm water. I like to use Dawn because it contains grease-cutting chemicals known as surfactants. Dampen a cloth (don't get it dripping wet) and wipe the surface in the same manner as before. Most of the grime and dirt is removed with this second step because the soapy water pulls off the oily residue from the first step and also removes water-soluble grime like sugary food spills. Change the cloth frequently to a clean part. When you're done, lightly wipe the surface using distilled water to remove any soap residue.

How to revive a wipe-on, oil-based finish

One of the most popular finishes used by non-professional woodworkers is some type of an oil finish. This includes pure tung oil or boiled linseed oil, one of the Danish oils, a wiping varnish, or an oil/varnish mix. All these finishes are popular because they penetrate deep into the wood, accentuate figure and detail, and provide a very natural, low-luster finish that woodworkers like.

A downside of these in-the-wood finishes is that over time they get dull and the wood loses its luster. The steps below are a good way to really liven these finishes back up. This was probably the first finish you used, and luckily for you, it is among the easiest to revive.

Wet-sand to remove minor scratches—You're bound to find minor surface scratches on pieces that have seen normal household use, but this next step should repair them. You'll need some type of

wiping varnish such as Seal-A-Cell, Waterlox Original, or Minwax Antique Oil. If you know the original finish was a pure tung or linseed oil and you want to avoid adding any kind of film finish, you can substitute Danish oil.

Pour a small puddle of the finish onto the surface and then use a small piece of wet-or-dry sandpaper (600-grit CAMI or P1000-grit FEPA) to wet-sand in circles or with the grain. Sand until any slight scratches are gone and the surface looks uniform. Remove the excess with a dry cloth and let it dry at least six hours.

These penetrating finishes aren't usually used with dyes or glazes, so you probably won't need to touch up any missing color

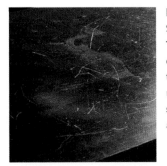

REVIVE LACQUER OR SHELLAC.
These thicker film finishes can be sanded smooth and then just waxed. Although unsightly, most surface scratches and dull areas are only skin deep.

Sand it smooth. Use 600-grit sandpaper to remove the damaged surface of the finish, leaving a more even appearance.

Retouch missing color. Any old piece that was originally dyed or stained is likely to need the color touched up. The edges of pieces are often worn down, revealing bare wood. A single brush stroke of color instantly restores their look. Combine different shades of furniture powders and some dewaxed shellac on a piece of white paper until you get a good match.

Finish with wax. After sanding away the damaged finish, apply a coat of paste wax and then polish it to an even sheen.

(see above), but if you do, let any color repairs dry for about an hour and then apply a coat of the same finish you used for wet-sanding. Using a small piece of paper towel or old cotton T-shirt, I apply just enough to make the surface look wet and then allow it to dry. Apply another coat or two if you want a deeper luster to the wood or more protection. As a final step, you can apply and buff out a coat of paste wax.

Sand and wax shellac or lacquer

Reviving a shellac or lacquer finish is even quicker because you don't have to add finish. You could, of course, as new shellac or lacquer will melt right into old, but it's easier to level what is already there than try to brush on a new, level coat. Do the two-step cleaning process, then instead of wet-sanding, dry-sand the finish lightly with P600-grit stearated sandpaper like Norton 3X or 3M Fre-Cut™. If the finish is slightly crazed (rough and cracked), sand it back as much as you can without sanding through to the stain or bare wood.

Touch up any missing color—If the piece was originally dyed or stained, or if you sanded through to lighter wood underneath, you may need to repair some colors. I mix dry furniture powders with SealCoat dewaxed shellac. You can blend a custom color and it dries very fast, so you can proceed to the next step without waiting. Use a No. 4 artist's brush (from art and crafts stores) and play with the colors on a piece of white paper until you get a reasonable match to the wood. Apply it sparingly, just enough to disguise the problem. Avoid the temptation to make it perfect because you are more likely to make the touch-up obvious.

Instead of more finish, I find that a coat or two of paste wax works better and is a lot easier. It adds a bit of luster and lends that silky feel that old furniture gets over time when it has been cared for. If you deliberately leave a little dark wax in corners and crevices, it adds an antiqued look. Always use tinted paste waxes on dark finishes. Clear wax can dry whitish and look bad on open-grained woods like oak.

Thick film finishes can only be cleaned

Film finishes like oil-based polyurethane, waterborne finishes, or high-tech, two-part finishes often found on kitchen cabinets don't revive very well. If you try to sand them, you are likely to go through a layer of finish and leave a witness line that can only be covered up by applying a new topcoat to the whole surface. However, these tough finishes are harder to damage, so there is a good chance that after the two-step cleaning they will be ready for many more years of useful service.

6 Finishing Fixes

MICHAEL MILLER

Some people enjoy finishing. A few might even prefer finishing furniture to building it. For the two of you who just said, "That's me!"—you're reading the wrong article. For most of us, finishing is a necessary evil: We need a great finish to bring out the best in our best, but we don't love the process and we dread a mistake. I've made more than my share of mistakes through the years, and I have picked up a few tips and tricks that will help you keep your sanity when the inevitable happens. I'll go from glue-up to touch-up, and by the end I hope you'll share my belief that everything (well, almost) is fixable, and you'll be able to approach your finishing with less fear and more fun. I know these tips will prove as useful to you as they have to me.

Repair, don't replace

Sometimes mistakes happen before you even begin finishing, but with the right repairs only you will know what happened. It's heartbreaking to drop a furniture component and see a piece crack or break off, but sometimes the chemical companies smile on us and develop the perfect product for a specific problem.

One such wonder is cyanoacrylate glue, which you probably know as "Super Glue." To repair a crack or split, simply squeeze a conservative amount of glue onto one of the pieces, push the two parts together, and spray on an activator. Also known as an accelerator, this catalyst comes in a pump bottle or an aerosol and speeds up the glue's setting. Wait a few seconds (the cure time will be different depending on the viscosity of the glue), and the pieces will be bonded. Unlike yellow glue, cyanoacrylate dries clear and very hard, so you can sand off the excess right away and it won't show under a clear finish. However, you'll need to dye or stain the piece before using this type of glue.

A super glue. Cyanoacrylate glue comes in different viscosities: Thin gets down into cracks, thick is good for vertical surfaces, and medium works well when gluing two parts where the glue can be applied to a horizontal surface, such as gluing cope-and-stick trim back on (left). While holding the two glued parts together (right), spray on the accelerator, which cures the glue instantly.

If you are dealing with a small piece, you can avoid getting glue on your skin by using a blunt but pointed tool as a clamp while you spray on the accelerator. This method also works on finished pieces, but use extreme care with the glue because you have to remove all the excess when you're finished and you don't want to have to apply more finish because of the repair.

Shopmade filler. Save sanding dust from your project and mix it with either lacquer or shellac to form a stiff filler.

Got gaps? Make some filler

Sometimes your joinery skills come back to haunt you with embarrassing gaps in tabletops or carcases. Even if you can clamp the gap closed, glue is unlikely to hold it. No problem, just fill it. Here's a simple recipe for the best sandable filler known to man. Collect fine sanding dust from the same wood as the piece you're repairing. Create a slurry using the sanding dust and a small amount of a fast-drying finish such as lacquer or dewaxed shellac. Simply force it into the joint as you would any other filler. The advantages to using a finish to make the filler (instead of the traditional choice of glue) are twofold: The paste dries faster and harder

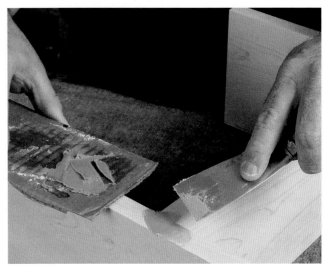

Fill the gap. Use a putty knife to force the filler into the open joint. The color difference will disappear when the filler dries and finish is applied.

Poor sanding revealed. An oil-based stain will reveal cross-grain scratches such as those on this frame.

Resand while wet. While the finish is still wet, sand the wood with the last grit you used (left) until all the cross-grain scratches are removed. Wipe more stain onto the bare wood (above) and blend it into the surrounding area.

than a glue-based one, and it contains the same combination of materials as the final product—finish and wood—so it's virtually invisible when used under a clear finish.

Removing sanding marks and glue stain

Poor sanding is the culprit behind a lot of poor finishes. Two main problems are swirl marks (from an orbital sander whose paper hasn't been changed frequently enough) and cross-grain scratches. Either problem may hide until a stain or a clear finish is applied. Don't panic. If you're using an oil-based stain or clear coat, sand with the grain while the finish is still wet, using the last grit you used. Sand until the scratches or swirl marks are gone. Then reapply the stain or finish and you should have no blending issues. If you're using a faster-drying finish, like lacquer or shellac, wait until the coat has dried, sand, and then reapply.

Another surface-preparation problem is dried glue, which is very easy to miss, especially on lighter woods. If you've missed some, use the same repair as you would on swirl marks. However, there is a great new product on the market to prevent this

Try fluorescent glue. A black light will reveal any traces left on the surface.

from happening. Franklin International's Titebond II Fluorescent Wood Glue contains a dye that shows up under a black light so that you can find every last trace of it during cleanup and sanding.

Shave away drips and runs

Don't rush your finishing. One of the most common mistakes is applying too much finish too fast, causing drips and runs. Then when you try to sand away the problem, you usually sand through the finish in the areas surrounding the drip or run. Meet your new best friend, the single-edged razor blade. It is, without a doubt, the most-used tool in my repair kit. For a drip or run, I use it as a miniature cabinet scraper. Just hold it between your thumbs and forefingers, flex it a little, and shave down the spot until it's level and glassy smooth.

There are several benefits to using a razor blade: Unlike sandpaper, which conceals the work area, a razor lets you see how much finish you are removing. The flex of the blade allows you to concentrate on the area you want to remove without disturbing the good finish surrounding it. Finally, a razor leaves a smooth surface that blends in with the next coat.

Touch-up for sand-through

When sanding an intermediate coat of finish, it's very easy to sand through the finish on corners and edges if you're not careful—and sometimes even if you are. If you've dyed or stained the wood, you now have the problem of matching the bare wood to the surrounding color. I do this with a couple of products.

My first choice is Mohawk's Blendal® sticks. Similar in shape to crayons, they are a soft wax blended with aniline dye as a coloring agent. You use the stick just like a crayon and lightly rub the surface with your finger to blend colors. These work great on edges, corners, and any other areas that need spot color adjustments. Don't leave the color too thick or it could invite adhesion problems. Instead, layer color and coats of lacquer or shellac until you've reached the required shade.

Drip tip. If you drip some finish onto a partially cured surface, don't try to wipe it off or blend it in. Instead, let it dry (above). Then use a single-edge razor blade like a cabinet scraper to bring the drip level with the surrounding surface.

Coloring pens. Blendal sticks come in many tones and can be used to touch up areas where you have sanded through the finish (center right). Eyeliner pencils can add color to small areas (bottom right).

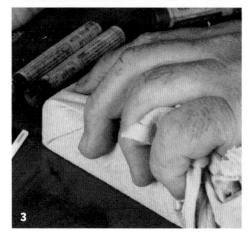

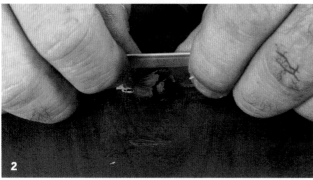

Fill and smooth. Colored wax sticks can be used to fill knot and nail holes after a finish has been applied (1). Use a razor blade to shave away the bulk of the surplus plug of wax (2). When the plug is almost level, switch to a credit card to bring it flush with the surface. Then wrap a cloth around a felt or cork-faced block and buff the plug and the surface to an even shine (3).

When Blendals aren't available, head to the drugstore's makeup department (yes, guys, I said makeup) and sort through the eyeliner and lip liners. They come in quite a few shades that match many finishes, and in the hands of a good finisher, they are like magic wands. Again, be careful not to apply too thick a layer.

Filling holes after finishing

To make repairs where the finish is already in place, I often use wax sticks. They come in many colors, making it easy to match the color of any finish. For small voids such as nail holes, simply rub the stick back and forth until the hole is filled and then wipe off the excess with a cloth.

For larger holes, cut a plug from the end of a stick and knead it until pliable. Next, press the lump of wax into the void, pushing it from side to side to ensure good adhesion. Now, return to your razor blade and start shaving away the excess until the wax is just above the surrounding surface. Switch to an old credit card or hotel room key card and scrape away the remaining surplus. Although slower than the razor blade, this won't damage the surrounding finish.

Give the wax a few minutes to harden and then, using a cloth wrapped around a cork-faced block, lightly buff the area to remove any wax from the adjacent wood and to bring up the shine. Wax sticks are great fillers but they are soft, limiting their use on high-traffic surfaces like tabletops.

Contributors

Greg Arceneaux is a professional furniture maker in Coventry, La.

Ben Blackmar is a former *Fine Woodworking* associate editor.

Sean Clarke is the owner of Clarke Restoration and Refinishing in Columbus, Ohio.

Jimmy Clewes is a professional turner in Las Vegas, Nev.

Michael Cullen is a studio furniture maker whose work can be seen at www.michaelcullendesign.com.

Peter Gedrys is a professional finisher and restorer in East Haddam, Conn. You can view his work at www.petergedrys.com.

Geoff Guzynski is a professional furniture maker near Chicago, Ill.

Reed Hansuld makes custom furniture in Brooklyn, N.Y.

Nancy Hiller builds custom furniture in Bloomington, Ind.

Jeff Jewitt lives in Cleveland, Ohio, and is a frequent writer on finishing. His latest book and DVD are *Spray Finishing Made Simple* (The Taunton Press, 2010). He is the owner of Homestead Finishing Products in Cleveland, Ohio.

Teri Masaschi is a professional finisher near Albuquerque, N.M., and teaches regularly across the country.

Scott McGlasson designs and builds furniture in St. Paul, Minn.

Michael Miller is a professional finisher near Nashville, Tenn.

Michael Pekovich is a furniture maker, instructor, and *Fine Woodworking*'s executive art director.

Mario Rodriguez is an instructor at the Philadelphia Furniture Workshop.

Mark Schofield was *Fine Woodworking*'s resident finishing expert for 13 years.

Vijay Velji is the owner of Shellac Finishes (www.shellacfinishes.com).

Credits

All photos are courtesy of *Fine Woodworking* magazine © The Taunton Press, Inc., except as noted below:

pp. 4–7: Why Finish Wood? by Mark Schofield, issue 215. Photos by Steve Scott, except for photo p. 4 by Kelly J. Dunton and left photo p. 6 and top photo p. 7 by Mark Schofield.

pp. 8–17: Fundamentals: The language of finishing Part 1 by Mark Schofield, issue 229 and Fundamentals: The language of finishing Part 2 by Mark Schofield, issue 232. Photos by *Fine Woodworking* staff.

pp. 18–24: A Pro's Secret to a Perfect Finish by Peter Gedrys, issue 253. Photos by Mark Schofield, except for photos p. 19 and bottom photo p. 21 by John Tetreault.

pp. 25–32: All Finishes Have a Shelf Life by Jeff Jewitt, issue 232. Photos by Mark Schofield, except for photos p. 25 by John Tetreault and top photo p. 31 by Jeff Jewitt.

pp. 33–38: Brushes for Woodworkers by Peter Gedrys, issue 236. Photos by Steve Scott, except for individual brush photos by John Tetreault.

pp. 39–46: Sanding Basics by Jeff Jewitt, issue 250. Photos by Mark Schofield.

pp. 47–53: Are You Sanding Right? by Teri Masaschi, issue 225. Photos by Mark Schofield.

pp. 54-59: A Closer Look: Sandpaper by Teri Masaschi, issue 228. Photos by Mark Schofield.

pp. 60-67: Sand between Coats for a Flawless Finish by Jeff Jewitt, issue 211. Photos by Mark Schofield, except for product shots by John Tetreault.

pp. 68-72: Easiest Finish? Danish Oil by Greg Arceneaux, issue 238. Photos by Matthew Kenney.

pp. 73-77: Get Better Results with Polyurethane by Ben Blackmar, issue 239. Photos by Steve Scott, except for photo p. 73 by John Tetreault.

pp. 78–84: Tabletop Finish with a Hand-Rubbed Feel by Mark Schofield, issue 214. Photos by Michael Pekovich, except for top photos and bottom left photo p. 81 by Matthew Kenney.

pp. 85–91: Wiping Varnishes? by Mark Schofield, issue 245. Photos by Asa Christiana, except for photos p. 90 and 91 by John Tetreault.

pp. 92–98: Wiping Varnish: The Only Finish You'll Ever Need by Michael Pekovich, issue 218. Photos by Steve Scott.

pp. 99–105: Make Shellac Your Go-To Finish by Mario Rodriguez, issue 234. Photos by Henry P. Belanger, except for product photos and finish sample photos by John Tetreault.

pp. 106–110: Fast Shellac Finish by Michael Pekovich, issue 256. Photos by Dillon Ryan, except for photo p. 106 and right photo p. 110 by Michael Pekovich. Drawing by Dan Thornton.

pp. 111–117: French Polishing Demystified by Vijay Velji, issue 217. Photos by Mark Schofield.

pp. 118–129: Antique Finish that Holds Nothing Back by Peter Gedrys, issue 220. Photos by Mark Schofield.

pp. 130–133: Lather Up by Reed Hansuld, issue 246. Photos by Jonathan Binzen.

pp. 134–141: All about Wax by Peter Gedrys, issue 191. Photos by Mark Schofield, except for photo p. 134 by Michael Pekovich and photos p. 135 and top 2 photos p. 136 by John Tetreault.

pp. 142–144: Designer's Notebook: Splash color on wood by Scott McGlasson, issue 252. Photos by Paul Nelson.

pp. 145–152: Better than Paint by Sean Clarke, issue 226. Photos by Mark Schofield.

pp. 153–158: A Closer Look: The hows and whys of dyes by Peter Gedrys, issue 217. Photos by Mark Schofield, except for photos p. 154 and 157 by Kelly J. Dunton.

pp. 159–163: Finish Line: Accentuate carving with color by Michael Cullen, issue 221. Photos by Mark Schofield.

pp. 164–168: Finish Line: Colorize your turning by Jimmy Clewes, issue 218. Photos by Mark Schofield.

pp. 169–171: Finish Line: Texture wood to highlight the grain by Geoff Guzynski, issue 233. Photos by Mark Schofield.

pp. 172–176: Finish Line: Traditional crackle finish by Nancy Hiller, issue 261. Photos by Jonathan Binzen, except for photo p. 172 by Kendall Reeves.

pp. 177–186: Get Started Spraying by Teri Masaschi, issue 248. Photos by Ben Blackmar, except for photos p. 178 and 179 by John Tetreault and photos p. 185 by Steve Scott. Drawings by John Tetreault.

pp. 187–193: Spray for Less by Teri Masaschi, issue 242. Photos by Ben Blackmar.

pp. 194–198: Switch to Spraying Water-Based Finishes by Teri Masaschi, issue 219. Photos by Mark Schofield.

pp. 199–204: Don't Overlook Aerosols by Teri Masaschi, issue 221. Photos by Mark Schofield. Drawings by *Fine Woodworking* staff.

pp. 205–211: Revive a Finish by Jeff Jewitt, issue 228. Photos by Mark Schofield.

pp. 212–216: 6 Finishing Fixes by Michael Miller, issue 214. Photos by Mark Schofield.

Index